T0146654

"If you want to begin living a life on purpose and better than you ever thought possible, read my friend Craig Sroda's Sweet Spot Workbook and see how fulfilling life can be by living in your natural strengths and wiring."

-PETE WALKEY
Author, The Lighthouse Leadership Principle

"Two crucial aspects of any written document that is published are validity of the information and the practicality of applying the findings. Craig's newest book definitely meets both of these requirements. He takes numerous effective tools that have been proven and combines them into a process that he used personally to become his best. Secondly, he provides a step-by-step process to discover your strengths and passion that will uncover your "Sweet Spot." This is applicable to all, whether in business or in other careers. A must use book."

-TONY HUTTI
CEO, Executive Forums Indiana

"Through life experiences, study and thoughtful guidance from mentors and friends, Craig Sroda learned the potential of purposeful living. In Your Sweet Spot he lays out a practical, step-by-step guide that will help you unlock the power of a life lived intentionally."

-TIM LEMAN
Chairman & CEO - Gibson

"I've known Craig for more than two decades with seven companies, six kids and two marriages between us. With a front row seat all these years, I've seen the impact Craig's intentional living has on those around him; professionally and personally. He's an authentic leader, working hard, openly learning from mistakes and generously sharing successes. Lean in and use this workbook up! Craig's done the hard work so your job can be easier and more rewarding."

- KEM MEYER
Communications Consultant and author of Less Chaos. Less Noise.

YOU in the SWEET SPOT

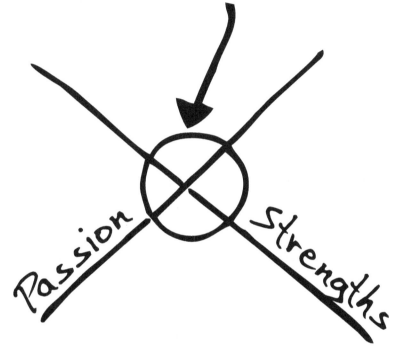

Know Your Strengths, Understand Your Why, Live on Purpose

A Strengths Based Approach for Life Planning

Craig C. Sroda

AuthorHouse™
1663 Liberty Drive
Bloomington, IN 47403
www.authorhouse.com
Phone: 1 (800) 839-8640

© 2016 Craig Sroda. All rights reserved.

No part of this book may be reproduced, stored in a retrieval system, or transmitted
by any means without the written permission of the author.

Published by AuthorHouse   09/08/2016

ISBN: 978-1-5246-2758-4 (sc)
ISBN: 978-1-5246-2757-7 (e)

Library of Congress Control Number: 2016914429

Print information available on the last page.

Any people depicted in stock imagery provided by Thinkstock are models,
and such images are being used for illustrative purposes only.
Certain stock imagery © Thinkstock.

This book is printed on acid-free paper.

Because of the dynamic nature of the Internet, any web addresses or links contained in this book may have changed
since publication and may no longer be valid. The views expressed in this work are solely those of the author and do
not necessarily reflect the views of the publisher, and the publisher hereby disclaims any responsibility for them.

Scripture quotations marked KJV are from the Holy Bible, King James Version (Authorized Version). First published
in 1611. Quoted from the KJV Classic Reference Bible, Copyright © 1983 by The Zondervan Corporation.

table of contents

FORWARD

Knowing your strengths. Understanding your why. Living on purpose. These are three keys to living life with balance, contentment and intentionality that Craig Sroda presents in his latest book.

His goal is to help people get to their sweet spot—the place where passions and strengths come together. When that happens, the magic happens. Life begins to feel different. It is lived out and experienced in a refreshing paradigm where the mind, body and spirit are renewed and rejuvenated because they are living with passion, purpose and a proactive plan.

Not too many things in life feel as good as being balanced. No amount of money, success, achievement or accumulation can bring true happiness. In fact, for many people these things only add frustration because they can become a major distraction by keeping a person away from carrying out the job, role or activities that are most important or fulfilling.

With no control, life becomes out of alignment. Values get buried. Your time becomes hostage to the things that have taken over like weeds in an unattended garden. I know this life well. I lived it. Most of us do at some time in our lives. I call this imbalance, or misalignment, the wobble effect.

Think of the spinning top. Younger people reading this might have to Google what that is. The top was a toy that spun on a pointed base by pulling a string and releasing it onto a hard surface. The top would spin nice and smooth because it was constructed to be balanced. But if you attached strings to the top that had various lengths and weights at the ends, the top would wobble. It would no longer be balanced until the strings and weights were adjusted to bring things back to balance. That's the wobble effect. That's what happens to us when we're out of alignment.

Craig addresses this head on by providing a guide that will help you to get your life back. You in the Sweet Spot is the life action plan and play book that gets rid of the wobble and brings about balance by navigating you through a process that exposes your strengths, weaknesses and passions. From that, you gain the knowledge it takes to put a plan in motion that will not only put you in your sweet spot, but will also keep you in your sweet spot.

I've known Craig Sroda for many years. I knew the hardcore-hard charging-high octane business Craig that grew a successful business enterprise, and I've seen the Craig I know today who is happier and more fulfilled by living out his true purpose everyday helping others to do the same as a certified life planner. When he asked me to design the cover for this book, I was very honored. When he selected me to write a foreword, I was more than honored because I believe full heartedly in what the content of this book can do for anyone that reads it and takes it seriously.

Craig put his knowledge, experience, passions and strengths into this book that provides insights and opportunities to grow by interacting with the pages. This is more than a book. It is a workbook. If you follow along and take the journey from beginning to end, you will have taken the first steps of the many that will keep you in your sweet spot.

SCOTT FRANKO,
Founder and Owner of Franko Design, LLC
Author of Lessons from a Pair of Old Gloves, Building Impressions and Pay Notes

First and foremost I would like to thank God. The journey of experiences he has provided for me has been rich beyond anything I could imagine. In the process of putting this book together it became very apparent the teachings He put me through in order to be more mature and complete so I could have a positive impact on those around me. The lessons I learned stretched me out of my comfort zone and provided a foundation for me to stand upon. Some of those lessons were whispered to me while at other times they flat out pushed me in the right direction. It was awesome.

To all of the friends, teachers and leaders that helped me through life by experiences, books, audiobooks, podcasts and even cassette tapes, including Tony Robbins, Kem Meyer, Mark Beason, Dave Ramsey, James Solomon, Michael Hyatt, Andy Stanley, my Pinnacle Colleagues, and my friends from the gym, community, and church, thank you. I am truly grateful.

To my wife, Tanna Mae. You are the best thing that has ever happened to me. You helped me navigate being a father, husband, friend and business leader. You are my #1 fan which I am so ever grateful. All the teachings in this book, and the good that it will provide to others, I owe you much of the credit. You were very influential on my direction in life along with the many accomplishments we did together. Thank you for believing in me, knowing we were put here for a bigger purpose, and holding my hand as we accomplished our goal of making our family generation better. I Love You Always and Forever!!!

To my daughters, Abby, Allison, Emily. You ladies are the best gift I could have ever received. You welcomed me into fatherhood which I am so thankful for. Through our experiences together you have helped me become a better man to which I hope to make this world a better place by helping others know their strengths and live on purpose. You have contributed to the ripple effect that this book can have in the world. I am grateful to all three of you as individual ladies. Your mom and I are always here for you as you start your new chapters in life. Enjoy the journey. I love you with all of my heart. You are three of the four people I would give my life for. Love You Guys - (Alpha, Bravo, Bravo, Yankee / Alpha, Lima, Lima, Indigo, Sierra, Oscar, November / Echo, Mike).

If there is anyone that I forgot, please forgive me as the purpose of this book is to help as many people know their strengths, know their why, and live on purpose to make a difference in the world while having fun.

YOUR SWEET SPOT
A Strengths Based Approach to Life Planning

This book is a strengths based approach to life planning and living on purpose for purpose. It can be used as a life planning book or used to help you be intentional about the next chapter of your life. You will need to understand the purpose of operating in your sweet spot and *knowing* what it is. Getting perspective on who you are and where you are in life from another view will allow you see farther and dial into your purpose. Fulfilling your unique role is the key to achieving personal satisfaction. When you are living the life you were meant to live, you will have a sense of purpose and joy.

Understanding what truly is important to you, what you stand for, and getting a grip on where you are in life right now will allow you to put an action plan together for you to live an intentional life. *You should not want to watch your days pass without you contributing to your purpose in life.* Unless you gain a full perspective on your life, and put a plan together for your life, you can miss the very purpose for your being.

After 18 years of starting a technology company, which ended up being the largest Microsoft partner in northern Indiana, I decided to sell it after I did my first life plan. It was a huge decision and something that was not taken lightly because I was coupled very tightly to it. It was a big part of my identity and breaking me away from the business was a huge step in the right direction for my life, my wife and family. I share this because like most young entrepreneurs I had some narcissism tendencies and my ego was, well, let's just say it was rather strong.

After doing my first life plan on my own and determining the business was going to take another big push by me to make it to the next level. Technology was taking some major shifts, mobile was allowing the workforce to be empowered in a new way which was going to take another set of skills to manage. After I determined my priorities in my life plan, it became apparent that if I was true to my priorities, I could not and did not want to put my wife and family through this next big push. I was 28 when I started Pinnacle in Indiana and it took its toll on my marriage and family as I simply could not be around nor was I mature enough to realize it. So the decision was done and to make a very complicated story simple, we sold the business.

So then the hard part. Who am I, what do I want to do, who do I want to be now? All questions I had to wrestle with as I pushed through the next few years of being part of a bigger company. I couldn't make all the decisions and further more felt handicapped to think and make a difference. My top 2 strengths are futuristic and strategic so I like to lead because I tend to see where things need to go and what is coming that we need to think about. Regardless of all that, decoupling my identity from the business was step one which was a tough one. Understanding my priorities definitely helped me through this sometimes dark time was extremely important for me to keep my sanity.

Defining my priorities, my core values, my mission and my why helped me to understand what I wanted to do next. It was to help people understand their strengths, live on purpose, and be better than they thought they could be.

One of the exercises that I did was the life wheel of balance. This is where you see how balanced your life is in the areas that you define as priorities. This helped me see where I was and helped me develop a plan to get back in balance and get to my sweet spot.

What is your "Sweet Spot" you ask? Simply put your sweet spot is where your natural strengths and passion intersect. Getting to this intersection will ultimately allow you to be a happier and more productive person. The premise is when you know your natural strengths, you operate in a natural state which consciously and unconsciously you are at ease.

This comfort zone allows you to breath easier, think easier, do you job better, encourage others around you, and ultimately have an influence that you normally would not have. When you are happier at work, which is a big part of our life, you go home happier which impacts your family and friends in a positive way, you impact your community beyond your family which can have a huge ripple effect. Just think of you having a positive impact on someone and the potential that can have on the others they come in contact with. So, see where this is going. Knowing your natural strengths can have huge impacts on the ones directly connected to you and the most powerful thing is you can influence outside your direct circle of influence.

No matter where you are in life, high school, college, teacher, professional, mother, dad, retired, your ring of influence is huge if you are intentional about you, then intentional about the life you want to look back and be happy with. No one goes through life thinking they are going to have regrets, but guess what – they do if they don't plan. The one thing my wife and my daughters have heard me say more than I care to mention is "You Don't Plan to Fail, You Fail to Plan". It is true, this journey you are about to embark on will help you be intentional about your life regardless of where you are so don't waste anymore time. Remember this, there are a lot of regrets people have when they look back at their life, but the top 2 that I know to be a fact are"

#2 – I Worked Too Much
#1 – I didn't have the courage to do what I wanted to do.

The journey begins now. Give yourself a break and let go of a destination you may of hand in your mind because you need to enjoy this journey which will make you stronger and more complete. If you don't quite get that read **James 1:2**

Consider it pure joy, my brothers and sisters, whenever you face trials of many kinds, because you know that the testing of your faith produces perseverance. Let perseverance finish its work so that you may be mature and complete, not lacking anything...

Our life is finite and there definitely is an end. Our job is to determine our sweet spot and be a productive positive person that is executing on why they were put here on earth. How you want to be remembered is up to you and you do have control of this. Our days are numbered, so take the time to prioritize the things that are important to you. When you live as if your days are numbered you will gain a heart of wisdom.

The Challenge to YOU is complete this book in its entirety and do all of the exercises outlined with an open mind and a desire to minimize any regrets in your life. I make this promise, if you do this with your heart and head connected, you will create a life plan that will bring you clarity and peace about you and your future.

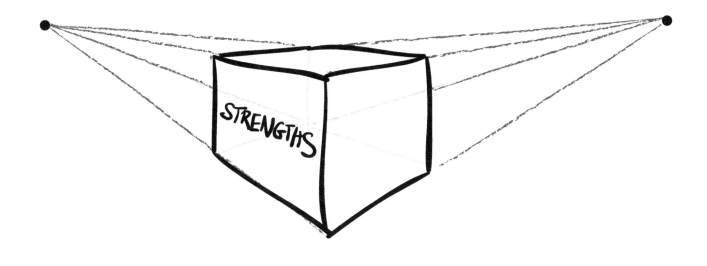

1 WHO ARE YOU?

Getting Perspective on Who You Are

> "See things in the present, even if they are in the future."
> – Larry Ellison

The most important thing you can do for you and the people you care about is get perspective on who you are. Understanding what your natural strengths are and what you are passionate about is probably the best gift you can give to yourself. If you know these foundational truths about yourself, you can truly make a difference in your life and have a major impact on the ones around you.

Whether you think you know your strengths or not, you should validate them. In today's world, not knowing your natural strengths and how you interact with the world around you is just keeping you away from the doors that open to new possibilities. It starts with knowing your natural strengths and how you are perceived by others. The theme here is to know your strengths, get perspective on you, understand where you will be the happiest and to have your biggest impact for yourself and others around you.

There are a lot of people I personally know that are not operating in their strengths zone or their sweet spot. There are also thousands of people that could be a lot happier and have much more influence helping others to their sweet spot if they had the tools to help them. The commitment I am making through this book is to help you operate at your best in life and have impact on others through the positive ripple affect you will have everyday.

Here is a quick test to see if you are operating out of your sweet spot. Check the boxes that apply.

☐ 1. I am dissatisfied with my work or home situation AND I haven't done anything to resolve it.
☐ 2. I tend to complain, blame others or have a cynical attitude.
☐ 3. I have one foot out the door, keeping my options open – but not acting on them.
☐ 4. I jump from job to job or assignment to assignment without making a difference.
☐ 5. My performance barely meets expectations.
☐ 6. I have trouble focusing on projects and find my mind wandering.
☐ 7. I don't have a plan for my next steps going forward.

If you answered Yes to any of the above, it is time for you to change and engage in the next version of you.

There are 4 key areas you should know about you to make a better, happier and healthy you.

1. Your 5 Natural Strengths
2. How The World Sees You
3. Your Emotional Intelligence Level
4. Your Love Tanks

You may know some or all of these, but getting them pulled together to get a real perspective on who you are will help you map out your ultimate life plan. It starts with the real assessments about yourself. Don't freak out. This is not a book of psychology or to psycho-analyze you. It is about getting to the facts about who you really are. Let's gets this journey started to capitalize on your strengths and maximize why you were brought into this world.

There are 4 assessments you must do and document. You must get comfortable with assessing yourself because this is about you. Not from an ego standpoint, but where your sweet spot is, where you can influence the most, and where you need to live to be the happiest.

"Those who used their talents saw them multiplied, and in the end, there were given even more talents and enlarged responsibility. The one who failed to use his talent had it stripped away." – Matthew 25:14-29.

We all have weaknesses, but we contribute through our gifts—our strengths. We need to make sure we have our weaknesses covered, but focusing on your strengths and gifts will allow you to operate in your most effective state.

Please do not back away from these assessments. They are about understanding you and could be the most important thing you have ever done for yourself.

YOUR STRENGTHS ASSESSMENT (Strengths Finder 2.0) by Gallup Research

The assessment I use and recommend is called strengths finder 2.0. Take the test and fill in the following template.

STRENGTHS ASSESSMENT
Here are the steps to taking the assessment.
1. Go to www.strengthsfinder.com
2. Sign up to take the assessment.
3. Setup an account
4. Take the test
5. Review Results by signing into the strengths finder portal (http://strengths.gallup.com)

a.Go To Reports
        b.View and Print – Strengths Insight and Action-Planning Guide
        c.View and Print – Strengths Insight Guide
6. Fill in your top 5 strengths.
7. Fill in the description of the strength from the Strengths Finder Strengths List from the end of this chapter.

Your Results – Strengths Assessment	
Top 5 Strengths	**Description**

The strengths finder results are what make you unique. Understanding these strengths and utilizing the reports you receive from Gallup's strengths assessment will help you make life decisions that are aligned with how you are naturally wired.

Take a moment and write down your key findings.

Key Learnings – Strengths Finder 2.0 Assessment
What Did You Learn?
What Stood Out?
What Was a Surprise?
What is in Question?

THE FASCINATION ASSESSMENT (HOW THE WORLD SEES YOU) by Sally Hogshead

I taught this course for many of people over the past few years. What I like about this course is it gives you another unique perspective on how others see you and what they see fascinating about you. Once you know how others see you, you can have a competitive advantage and a stronger influence with others to help you accomplish whatever you are targeting. This could allow you to have deeper conversations with friends, a stronger relationship with your spouse, children, co-workers, employees and even the people you directly report to.

This is not some form of manipulation, this is knowing how you are being received by others and you will understand what your unique advantage is so you can stay in your sweet spot. Harnessing this power to focus on your archetypes will allow you to confidently say yes to things that are not an area of strength for you and allow you to standout and transform your life or career. Fascinate in ancient Latin is facsinare which means to bewitch or hold captive so people are powerless to resist. Again, this is not a manipulation tactic, but to help you be more productive with how you are naturally wired. There are 7 primary fascination advantages and for most people there are 2 advantages where they communicate most confidently and effortlessly.

The 7 Fascination Advantages:
• **Innovation:** Creative brainstormers
• **Passion:** Relationships builders with strong people skills
• **Power:** A leader who makes decisions
• **Prestige:** Over achievers with higher standards
• **Trust:** Stable and reliable
• **Mystique:** Solo intellect behind the scenes
• **Alert:** Precise detail manager

The combination of your primary and secondary advantage are what create your archetype. Once you know your archetype, you can open the door to harnessing your best self.

FASCINATION ASSESSMENT

Here are the steps to taking the assessment.
1. Go to www.howtheworldseesyou.com/you
2. Setup an account
3. Use the code "entreleadership"
4. Take the assessment
5. Watch the video
6. Document and Print Express Assessment Report
7. Fill in your results below

If you want to purchase the full assessment.
1. Go to www.howtofascinate.com
2. Go To Individual and the drop down menu will appear
3. Click Fascination Advantage Express Assessment & Report
4. Purchase the Assessment.
5. Watch the video
6. Print the report and follow instructions
7. Fill in your results below

Your Results – Fascination Assessment	
Archetype	**Advantages**
Archetype: Your 3 Adjectives:	Primary Advantage: Secondary Advantage: Dormant Advantage:

Your Highest Value	Not Your Highest Value

Take a moment and write down your key take learnings.

Key Learnings – Fascination Assessment
What Did You Learn?
What Stood Out?
What Was a Surprise?
What is in Question?

EMOTIONAL INTELLIGENCE

Do you know The True Value of Emotional Intelligence? Recently I had to pull Emotional Intelligence by Daniel Goleman off my bookshelf. I have three daughters, two female dogs, and one male Shih-Tzu. Needless to say there isn't a lot of testosterone around my house. I wouldn't trade anything for the world, just stating the facts.

Allison, one of my daughters was having an issue regulating her responses so I decided to quickly educate her on Emotional Intelligence (EI). I thought it might be good for her to learn how to respond when she gets upset. It was an educational opportunity, so I shared my explanation of EI with her. How I explained this to her can be broken down into 5 classifications:

1. **Self-awareness** – You recognize your own emotions and how they affect your thoughts and behavior, know your strengths and weaknesses, and self-confidence.
2. **Self-Regulation** – Your ability to control impulsive feelings and behaviors, manage your emotions in healthy ways, take initiative, follow through on commitments, and adapt to changing circumstances.
3. **Social Skills and Awareness** – You can understand the emotions, needs, and concerns of other people, pick up on emotional cues, feel comfortable socially, and recognize the power dynamics in a group or organization.
4. **Relationship Management/Motivation** – You know how to develop and maintain good relationships, communicate clearly, inspire and influence others, work well in a team, and manage conflict.
5. **Empathy** – the ability to empathize with others and put yourself in their position.

If you have high emotional intelligence you are able to recognize your own emotional state and the emotional states of others, and engage with people in a way that draws them to you. You can use this understanding of emotions to relate better to other people, form healthier relationships, achieve greater success at work, and lead a more fulfilling life.

My question to you is how are you doing in the 5 areas? Do you know? The reason I ask is that Emotional Intelligence is important because it affects:

1. Your performance at work
2. Your physical health
3. Your mental health
4. Your relationships

To improve your emotional intelligence and your decision-making abilities, it's important to understand and manage your emotions. This can be accomplished by developing key skills for controlling and managing overwhelming stress and becoming effective at communication.
There are basically 5 skills to work on:

1. The ability to quickly reduce stress in a moment in a variety of settings.
2. The ability to recognize your emotions and keep them from overwhelming you.
3. The ability to connect emotionally with others by using nonverbal communication.
4. The ability to use humor and play to stay connected in challenging situations.
5. The ability to resolve conflicts positively and with confidence.

EMOTIONAL INTELLIGENCE QUOTIENT ASSESSMENT

There are many test on this. The key is to take a few and get a rating on how self-aware of you and of others you truly are. Try these test below and document your results:
Here are the steps to taking the assessment.
1. Take 1 or all 3 of these EI assessments and document your results:
    • http://greatergood.berkeley.edu/ei_quiz/
    • http://www.ihhp.com/free-eq-quiz/
    • http://testyourself.psychtests.com/testid/3038
2. Document your results below.
3. Document key learnings below

Your Score: 17/20

Nice work. You seem naturally well-attuned to others' emotions--a vital skill for forming compassionate connections. You scored well above average but still have room for growth; research suggests that people can improve their emotion recognition skills with practice. So keep an eye out for our forthcoming empathy training tool, designed to boost your emotional intelligence. Sign up for our e-newsletter for updates on it.

My GreaterGood results from Berkeley.edu

Your Results – Emotional Intelligence	
Test	**Score/Description**

Key Learnings – Emotional Intelligence
What Did You Learn?
What Stood Out?
What Was a Surprise?
What is in Question?

YOUR LOVE TANKS

Do you know what fills your love tank? The thing your spouse or friend that does that fills you up with love and joy? Most of us grow up learning the language of our parents, which was a literal thing or what they actually said coming from their mouth. I read a book by Gary Chapman called "The Five Love Languages" about 10 years into my marriage it was a game changer. I thought I was doing the right things to show my wife I was loving her but it ended up that I was wrong. 10 years of time of not knowing what my wife's love language was is a long time. I thought it was tasks as known as acts of service.

The premise is we all have a primary love language, something that fills our love tank so we consciously and unconsciously know we are loved. There are five ways to express love are:

1. **Words of Affirmation** – People with this love language greatly appreciate hearing compliments and encouraging words. They feel loved through what they hear and are pushed away by harsh criticisms.

2. **Quality Time** – People with this love language prefer undivided attention and plenty of time with their loved ones. They feel loved when they have lots of time invested in them, but for people with this love language, absence certainly doesn't make the heart grow fonder.

3. **Receiving Gifts** – People with this love language appreciate receiving presents and the thoughts behind them. They feel loved when they are given gifts spontaneously and are greatly offended when special occasions are forgotten or a thoughtless gift is given.

4. **Acts of Service (Task)** – People with this love language prefer their loved ones to perform meaningful and thoughtful acts. It could be as simple as washing the dishes or mowing the lawn, but they appreciate it and feel valued by such deeds. However, they feel unappreciated when they work on a task while their partner just watches without offering to help.

5. **Physical Touch** – People with this love language greatly appreciate simple gestures like holding hands, hugs or a touch on the arm. It's not just about sex, it's about knowing that you're there and that you love them. An absence of physical contact has the potential to significantly damage relationships with people who have this love language.

Do you know which one fills your tank, does one stand out that is number 1 to you? For many years I thought my wife's love tank was tasks. I would do things around the house, fix stuff, buy her stuff and so on. After reading the book and discussing the concept of love tanks with her, I now know that her love tank is quality time. It really did change our relationship because now I could make sure her love tank was getting filled. As you can imagine, if your love tank is empty problems occur and they are usually big ones.

5 LOVE LANGUAGES ASSESSMENT
Circle the answer that best applies to you.

1. A. I like to receive notes of affirmation.
   E. I like to be hugged.

2. B. I like to spend one-to-one time with a person who is special to me.
   D. I feel loved when someone gives practical help to me.

3. C. I like it when people give me gifts.
   B. I like leisurely visits with friends and loved ones.

4. D. I feel loved when people do things to help me.
   E. I feel loved when people touch me.

5. E. I feel loved when someone I love or admire puts his or her arm around me.
   C. I feel loved when I receive a gift from someone I love or admire.

6. B. I like to go places with friends and loved ones.
   E. I like to high-five or hold hands with people who are special to me.

7. C. Visible symbols of love (gifts) are very important to me.
   E. I feel loved when people affirm me.

8. E. I like to sit close to people whom I enjoy being around.
   A. I like for people to tell me I am beautiful/handsome.

9. B. I like to spend time with friends and loved ones.
   C. I like to receive little gifts from friends and loved ones.

10. A. Words of acceptance are important to me.
    D. I know someone loves me when he or she helps me.

11. B. I like being together and doing things with friends and loved ones.
    A. I like it when kind words are spoken to me.

12. D. What someone does affects me more than what he or she says.
    E. Hugs make me feel connected and valued.

13. A. I value praise and try to avoid criticism.
    C. Several small gifts mean more to me than one large gift.

14. B.   I feel close to someone when we are talking or doing something together.
    E. I feel closer to friends and loved ones when they touch me often.

15. A. I like for people to compliment my achievements.
    D. I know people love me when they do things for me that they don't enjoy doing.

16. E. I like to be touched as friends and loves ones walk by.
    B. I like it when people listen to me and show genuine interest in what I am saying.

17. D. I feel loved when friends and loved ones help me with jobs or projects.
    C. I really enjoy receiving gifts from friends and loved ones.

18. A. I like for people to compliment my appearance.
    B. I feel loved when people take time to understand my feelings.

19. E. I feel secure when a special person is touching me.
    D. Acts of service make me feel loved.

20. D. I appreciate the many things that special people do for me.
    C. I like receiving gifts that special people make for me.

21. B. I really enjoy the feeling I get when someone gives me undivided attention.
    D. I really enjoy the feeling I get when someone helps me make decisions.

22. C. I feel loved when a person celebrates my birthday with a gift.
    A. I feel loved when a person celebrates my birthday with meaningful words.

23. C. I know a person is thinking of me when he or she gives me a gift.
    D. I feel loved when a person helps with my chores.

24. B. I appreciate it when someone listens patiently and doesn't interrupt me.
    C. I appreciate it when someone remembers special days with a gift.

25. D. I like knowing loved ones are concerend enough to help with my daily tasks.
    B. I enjoy extended trips with someone who is special to me.

26. E. I enjoy kissing or being kissed by people with whom I am close.
    C. I enjoy receiving a gift given for no special reason.

27. A. I like to be told that I am appreciated.
    B. I like for a person to look at me when we are talking.

28. C. Gifts from a friend or loved one are always special to me.
    E. I feel good when a friend or loved one touches me.

29. D. I feel loved when a person enthusiastically does some task I have requested.
    A. I feel loved when I am told how much I am needed.

30. E. I need to be touched every day.
    A. I need words of encouragement daily.

Totals: A: B: C: D: E:

A. Words of Affirmation
B. Quality Time
C. Receiving Gifts
D. Acts of Service
E. Physical Touch

Your Results – Love Language	
Love Language	**Description**

Key Learnings – Love Language

What Did You Learn?

What Stood Out?

What Was a Surprise?

What is in Question?

HOW TO RELATE TO A PERSON WITH THIS LOVE LANGUAGE	COMMUNICATION	ACTION	WHAT TO AVOID
Words of Affirmation	Compliments Affirmations Kind Words	Send notes or cards	Criticism
Quality Time	One-on-one time Not interrupting Face-to-face conversation	Take long walks together Do things together Take Trips	Long periods of being apart. More time with friends than with partner.
Receiving Gifts	Positive, fact-oriented information	Give gifts on special occasions and also on not so special occasions	Forgetting special days
Acts of Service	Action words like "I can," "I will," "What else can I do?"	Helping with the house and yard chores. Repair/maintence. Acts of kindness.	Ignoring partner's request's while helping others.
Physical Touch	A lot of non-verbal. Verbal needs to be "word pictures."	Touches/Pats Hugs Kisses	Physical neglect or abuse

CHAPTER 1 SUMMARY

At this point I am hopeful you have gained some valuable insights about yourself, your naturals strengths, how others see you, your emotional intelligence, and your love language. Knowing these areas of your life is the first step toward achieving personal growth, satisfaction and happiness. I believe as you continue to discover who you are and how to grow in your natural strengths and wiring, you will come to know your greatest joy and be fulfilled like you never knew was possible.

The most important thing you can do for you and the people you care about is get perspective on who you are.

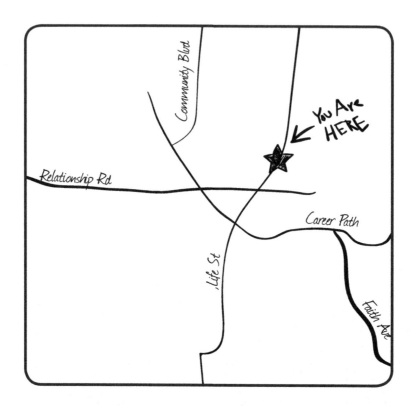

2 WHERE ARE YOU NOW?

Discovering Your New Starting Line

"The path to success is to take massive, determined action."
– Tony Robbins

Now that you have a better understanding and perspective of your strengths and how you are wired, its time to determine where you are now. To set the stage for this journey, it is a good idea to take stock of where you are in all domains of your life.

My wife and I recently completed our life plans by a certified life coach from the Patterson Center. This was my second life plan that helped me refine my mission and update my action plan. I like the quote from Winston Churchill "Plans are nothing; planning is everything." This is a good reminder that planning must take place to accomplish who we want to be and what we want to achieve in life.

The second life plan process was a rigorous 2-day process that challenged us to think deeper than we have in a while. Thinking about our legacy, our passions, our natural wirings, and documenting how we got to become who we are today is a rewarding exercise. Part of our plan was to get LifePlan certified. And we did it. We did it so that we can help others live intentionally and on purpose.

Reviewing and planning for all the domains in your life is something that I feel everyone should do. There are a few variations on the number of domains of life, but I feel most of them fall into major categories with a few subcategories for clarification. It's a good idea for you to measure how you are doing in each of them just to get a visualization on where you are. If one of the domain scores is low, your life may have a flat spot which will eventually affect you in a negative way. When your life domains are balanced like a wheel, life seems to "roll" a lot easier—like a wheel rolling down the road. When there is a flat spot in your life, your wheel will always hit that flat spot when you are rolling through life.

I did some digging and it turns out the wheel of life originated with Buddha in about 500 B.C. to assess a person's inner psychological state. The Wheel of Life has had a few names over the years like wheel of balance, wheel of happiness, etc. Bottom line; it can help you identify if you have a flat spot in your life.

My earlier life wheel examples are below. As you can see, at that time of my life with no life plan and heavy into career mode, I was out of balance. Life Plan #1 with action plans definitely got me going in the right direction. The most current assessment with Life Plan #2 is substantially improved.

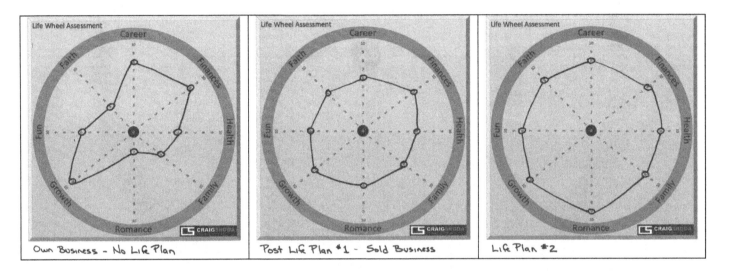

As you can see, I had flat spots when I was heavy in my career and working too much. When I was in this stage, I had many flat spots because I didn't classify my life into these domains AND I didn't have a life plan. I had a business and finance plan, but not a life plan. After my first life plan, along with selling the business, my life domains got a lot better. Today with an updated life plan and a mission defined with my wife, I am more aware of the life domains and the importance of having them in balance.

Clarify your present state with the Wheel Assessment. It's time to do your assessment and see if you have any flat spots in your life. This is an important step because you must know where you are before you start charting your course with the appropriate action plans.

WHEEL OF LIFE ASSESSMENT

Here are the steps to taking the assessment.
1. Each spoke on the wheel represents a facet of your present life.
2. Circle a number for 1 (low) to 10 (high) on each spoke, corresponding to the quality of each spoke's present state in your life.
3. Start on any spoke and continue clockwise around the wheel. Rate all spokes in 1 minute or less.
4. After rating all spokes, connect your rating numbers, as in the example below (need example)
5. Circle the two lowest-rated spokes. These are areas that need to be addressed.

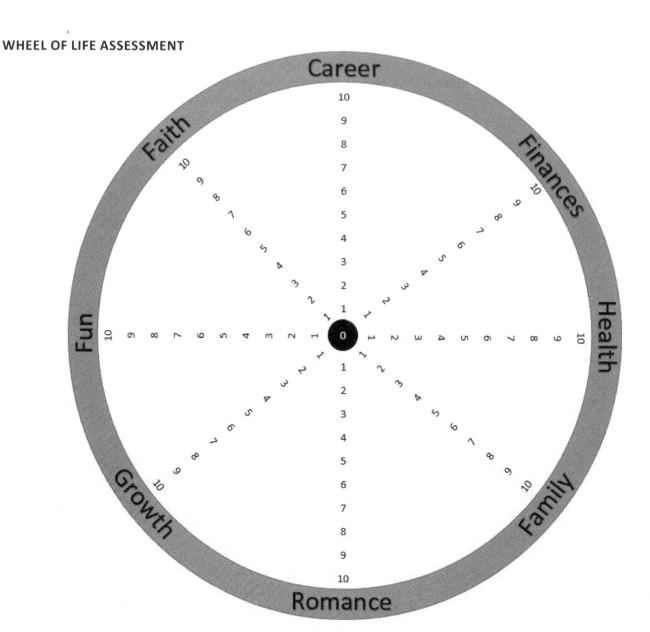

Key Learnings – Wheel of Life Assessment
What Did You Learn?
What Stood Out?
What Was a Surprise?
What is in Question?

This exercise should have revealed how balanced your life domains are in comparison to each other. If there is a flat spot it will continue to cause issues in your other domains. You can't fix this overnight, but you can come up with action plans to address low domain areas which we will talk about in later chapters.

TURNING POINTS

The last part of knowing where you are is understanding how you got here. What turning points in your life did you go through that made you – you. I remember Andy Stanley talking about raising children and our desire to give them more than we had. He said something that stuck with me which was, "you want to give them more than you had, but don't leave out the experiences you had that made you – you." I discussed that with my wife that night and we were able to have a lot of conversation around this because I felt sometimes I was not giving our daughters the very things that made us – us. There is a balance there because all of us have stuff we want to protect our family and friends from, but we need to challenge ourselves to keep the very core beliefs and things that made us who we are today so we pass those along to our family and the people we are trying to influence for good.

An important exercise to charting how you got to where you are today is understanding and documenting your milestones, major events, and experiences that opened and closed chapters of your life journey to date. These events will be good, bad, and sometimes emotional, but it is important to get them outlined so you have a firm grasp of your foundation you have today.

These turning points will be charted across your domains so when we start working on your life plan, the turning points along with the life wheel can help guide us with your next steps in each of the life domains.

The first step is to utilize the form below and list out what you know are your turning points with your age and the life domain(s) it impacted.

Make sure you allocated enough time for the next two sections.

TURNING POINT LIST ASSESSMENT
Here are the steps to taking the assessment.
1. Think about your turning points in life, something that affected you or turned your life in a significant way.
2. Write your age in the age column.
3. Write the details of that point.
4. List the life domains it impacted.

Here is my Turning Point list for Reference

TURNING POINTS

Age	Specifics	Life Domain(s)
15	Mom Passed Away	
18	Kicked Out of House Managed Hardware Store – James Solomon	
20	Got Associates Degree	
21	First Full-Time Job: Housing Allowance Bought House	
23	BS at Bethel – No One Showed	
24	Started at Crowe	
25	Bryan Aown Opened Bible to Me/ GCC Married to Tanna	
26	Abby Born/Family	
27	Baptized with Family	
28	Business Start- Up	
38	Poor Life Decisions	
39	Faith Re-Engaged (Mark)	
41	New Leadership Awareness (Kem CD)	
43	Hyatt Life Plan	
45	Sold Business	
47	Renewed Vision for Relationship w/ Tanna	

© Paterson Center, LLC.

Turning Point List		
Age	Specifics	Life Domain(s)

Now that you identified your turning points, it's time to put these into a timeline by domains. Use the Matrix below to map out your turning points.

TURNING POINT MATRIX AND INSTRUCTIONS
1. Count how many turning points you have from your list above
2. Print out the appropriate number of the turning points matrix below to allow you to put them across the top,
3. Fill in the turning points at the top
4. Write in your age
5. Write in details of the impact it had in each of the domain boxes. Note: not all the domains are affected for each turning point.

Turning Points Matrix				
Turning Points				
Age				
Career				
Finances				
Health				
Family				
Romances				
Growth				
Fun				
Faith				

When you are done with this task, see if you notice any themes that group your turning points together. For me as shown in the chart below, I could group many of my turning points into groups. My journey ended up being like this. (You can see full examples of my Turning Point profiles on the next page)

1. Survive
2. Strive
3. Grow
4. Blow Up
5. Rebuild
6. Relaunch
7. and I am in this phase with is to use these experiences to help others…

Highs		Managed Hardware Store	Got Associates Degree	First Full-Time Job	Bought House	Graduated From Bethel	Started at Crowe	Bryan Aown Opened Bible	Married Tana	Family Started	Baptized with Family	Business Start Up		New Leadership Awareness	Faith Re-Engaged	Hyatt Life Plan	Sold Business	Renewed Relationship w/ Tanna
Age		Teens					Twenties							Thirties		Forties		
Lows	Mom Passed Away	Kicked Out of House										Poor Life Decisions						
Themes		Survive			Strive			Grow					Blow Up		Rebuild		Relaunch	

© Paterson Center, LLC.

You should put your themes side by side, possibly even tape them together and group them like I did.

Key Learnings – Turning Points Matrix
What Did You Learn?
What Stood Out?
What Was a Surprise?
What is in Question?

Chapter Notes and Key Learning Points

Theme	Survive			Strive				
Turning Points	Mom Passed Away (1981, 15)	Kicked Out of House (1985, 18)	Managed Hardware Store (1985, 18)	Got Associates Degree (1987, 20)	First Full-Time Job (1988, 21)	Bought House (1988-89, 21)	Graduated from Bethel (1991, 23)	Started at Crowe (1991, 24)
Personal	Loss, Had to Work vs. Play, Independence Kicked Off	Motivated – "Had to Get After It"	Listened to Tony Robbins & Other CD's	Moved to Next Level – New Milestone	Financial Relief, "Moved Up a Wrung," Eye Opening to White Collar	Felt Success/ Independent	Huge Achievement	Financial Step: 23-24K, Bought 2nd House
Family	Foundation Broken	Lived with Grandma, Cause Divide in Family – Held Grudge w/ Dad & Stepmom						Met Tanna
Vocational	Had to Get a Job (Martin's)	Motivated, Had to Earn More	Huge Learning Curve – Learning a "Trade" – Mechanical, Taught Mechanical Lessons		1st Full Time Job: $16,000			Big Step – Learned Management, Teamwork, Computer Skills, Innovation, Dots Connecting
Church		Usher at Church w/ Grandma, Some Sunday Consistency	James Solomon Kept Faith Visible – Opened Bible				Got First Big Bible – Didn't Know What It Meant	Kem/Don GCC, Connections, Don Sharing Faith
Community								1st "Give-Back" Initiatives

© Paterson Center, LLC.

Theme	Grow				Blow Up		
Turning Points	Bryan Aown Opened Bible (1992, 25)	Married Tanna (1992, 25)	Family Started (1992-96, 26)	Baptized with Family (1995, 27)	Business Start-Up (1996, 28)	Poor Life Decisions (1998-07, 30-39)	New Leadership Awareness (2007, 39)
Personal		Learning How to Share Life	Responsibility Realization Kicked-In, Financial Pressure		Stress, Ego Kicked In, Money Focus, Independence, Out-of-Balance	Drinking/ Alcohol, Narcissism Diagnosis, Bad Decision	New "Ah-Ha"
Family		Life Partner!	Tanna at Home Decision, Built 1st House (3rd House)	Tanna & I Decided Faith Part of Family	Gone a Lot, MIA, Strain on Relationship	Relationship w/ Tanna Lowest Point, Swapped Money for Time	
Vocational			Became a Manager – Still on Radar to Grow/Step Every 3 Years, Learned GP		Learnings: Sales, Consulting, General Business, Accounting, Account Management	Driven to Hit Numbers	CD From Kem – Andy Stanley
Church	Started Reading Bible, Small Group w/ Don	GCC Steps Together, Volunteering		External Step	Went Down	Started Tithing	New Faith Awareness
Community							

© Paterson Center, LLC.

Theme	Survive			Strive				
Turning Points	Mom Passed Away (1981, 15)	Kicked Out of House (1985, 18)	Managed Hardware Store (1985, 18)	Got Associates Degree (1987, 20)	First Full-Time Job (1988, 21)	Bought House (1988-89, 21)	Graduated from Bethel (1991, 23)	Started at Crowe (1991, 24)
Personal	Loss, Had to Work vs. Play, Independence Kicked Off	Motivated – "Had to Get After It"	Listened to Tony Robbins & Other CD's	Moved to Next Level – New Milestone	Financial Relief, "Moved Up a Wrung," Eye Opening to White Collar	Felt Success/ Independent	Huge Achievement	Financial Step: 23-24K, Bought 2nd House
Family	Foundation Broken	Lived with Grandma, Cause Divide in Family – Held Grudge w/ Dad & Stepmom						Met Tanna
Vocational	Had to Get a Job (Martin's)	Motivated, Had to Earn More	Huge Learning Curve – Learning a "Trade" – Mechanical, Taught Mechanical Lessons		1st Full Time Job: $16,000			Big Step – Learned Management, Teamwork, Computer Skills, Innovation, Dots Connecting
Church		Usher at Church w/ Grandma, Some Sunday Consistency	James Solomon Kept Faith Visible – Opened Bible				Got First Big Bible – Didn't Know What It Meant	Kem/Don GCC, Connections, Don Sharing Faith
Community								1st "Give-Back" Initiatives

© Paterson Center, LLC.

When there is a flat spot in your life, your wheel will always hit that flat spot when you are rolling through life.

3 WHAT IS IMPORTANT TO YOU?

Core Values

"Don't be afraid to give up the good to go for the great."
– John D. Rockefeller

Have you sat down and truly defined what is important to you? Do you know your core values and what you stand for? In order to live on purpose and support what is important to you, these are decisions that need to be made by digging down deep inside of yourself.

Without knowing your core values and what you stand for, you will be in a state of confusion, and potentially chaos. These values are like your foundation that your house is built on. When your values disintegrate, everything around you disintegrates because you and your actions are not in sync with your belief system or core values. This is also known as cognitive dissonance.

Cognitive dissonance is "the mental stress or discomfort experienced by an individual who holds two or more contradictory beliefs, ideas, or values at the same time, or is confronted by new information that conflicts with existing beliefs, ideas, or values". Wow, that is a mouth full.

In today's technology and interconnected world, we are getting introduced to new ideas and other beliefs at crazy speeds. It is more important than ever to know what you stand for, your beliefs and your foundation.

Take a step back from trying to understand your core values and simply answer this question: Do I know what I will absolutely say YES and NO to? If not, which is normal, it is time to define your core values.

One important fact you must keep in the foremost of your mind is that as you get into this process of identifying, clarifying, and writing down your core values, it is not a single event. You do not do this one-time and forget about it, this is a dynamic and evolutionary process. In order to start the process of defining your core values, you have to open your mind to new possibilities of thinking.

Remember this; *"Your mind is like a parachute – it only works when it is open."*

Here are some questions and exercises get you ready.

1. **Are you playing an infinite or finite game of life?**
    a. Finite games have a definite beginning and ending. There are rules with the goal of someone winning and the game ending.
    b. Infinite games do not have a beginning or ending. They are viewed as a game of continual play and sometimes bring others into the game.
2. **Do you live as if your days are numbered?**
    a. When you plan out your days, weeks, years, do you have the attitude that you have a specific number of days left here are earth?
    b. Do you prioritize the appropriate tasks as your days are numbered?

These are not fun questions, but very real. In fact, we do have a specific number of days here on earth. We all do. Understanding this should be a driver for you to live on purpose for a purpose as it is defined by you. If you are feeling a bit overwhelmed or unsure where to start – you are not alone. Defining your core values is a hard thing to do because they are deep inside of you and you may not have the words easily to describe them. In order to get your mind ready for the one action item below which is defining your core values, work through and write down thoughts around these questions.

Core Values Warm Up Exercise Questions

1. **What are your life roles?**
    (Examples: parent, spouse, manager, coach, brother, sister, son, daughter, manager, etc.)

2. **What things seem most important about each of your life roles?**

3. **What people, things, or activities seem most important to me?**

4. When you don't have pressure in your life, what do you like to do?

5. If you only had 90 days to live, what would you do?

6. When my life is over:
    a. What will you be glad you did?
    b. What would you like your obituary to say about you?

7. What do you really do well?

8. Is there something you feel you should do but haven't had the courage to do?

The biggest question is which of the above questions do you really want? Not what others are expecting of you, or have set in place for you, but what your heart and head is telling you is the most important. When you are defining your core values it is important to think of them as your belief system. Your purpose in life may change or take on a new meaning but your core values should be timeless and unchanging. As you go through life you may want to tweak the words to be more meaningful, but the core of the core value should be what you stand for and the foundation of who you are.

My core values are:
1. Learn Forever
2. Have Fun
3. Make a Difference
4. Help Others
5. Respect Others
6. Keep Truth and Faith as My Foundation

Let's get started working on your core values. The following "Core Values Worksheet" will help you start putting your values to paper. It is very important in the second column to answer both questions for each role. That "what" is important and the "why" this is important. You should ask the "why" a 3-5 times for each to yourself.

CORE VALUES WORKSHEET INSTRUCTIONS
1. List your roles in the roles column.
2. Write what is important to you about this role.
3. Write down 3 to 5 statements of why this is important to you
4. Repeat this process for all your roles

5. Start back at the top and determine if there are common words or themes in your what and why's that can allow you to formulate a couple core value words or short statements.
    a. You do not have to have a core value for each role, because your foundation may cover multiple areas or roles in your life.
6. Use the My Core Values worksheet to narrow your core values to 5 to 6 words or short statements.
7. Now the fun part—you have to test your values.
    a. Identify situations where your core values can potentially hurt you. Like having a core value of innovation but you thrive on stability vs. constant change. If you can't think of a case where the value steers you wrong, you probably have a keeper.
8. Validate your core values with a trusted friend.
    a. Remember, they are your core values so be careful you don't make someone else's thoughts become yours because this is your life.

> **As Mahatma Ghandi said,**
> *"Your beliefs become your thoughts.*
> *Your thoughts become your words.*
> *Your words become your actions.*
> *Your actions become your habits.*
> *Your habits become your values.*
> *Your values become your destiny."*

This process will require focused time and thought. It is best to do this exercise with another person you trust if possible. Talking out loud and hearing what you are thinking can be very helpful. Using the worksheets can detangle thoughts in your mind because things get clear through your finger tips and pencil tips.

Core Values Worksheet		
Role	**What's Important About This Role?** **Why is it Important?**	**Core Value**

Core Values Worksheet (CONT.)		
Role	What's Important About This Role? Why is it Important?	Core Value

Core Values and Behaviors Worksheet

Core Value

Specific, Observable Behaviors that Demonstrate Your Core Value and Belief

Core Value

Specific, Observable Behaviors that Demonstrate Your Core Value and Belief

Core Value

Specific, Observable Behaviors that Demonstrate Your Core Value and Belief

Core Value

Specific, Observable Behaviors that Demonstrate Your Core Value and Belief

Core Value

Specific, Observable Behaviors that Demonstrate Your Core Value and Belief

Core Value

Specific, Observable Behaviors that Demonstrate Your Core Value and Belief

My Core Values

Core Value

Core Value

Core Value

Core Value

Core Value

Core Value

These values are my foundation and what I will live my life by.

Your purpose in life may change or take on a new meaning but your core values should be timeless and unchanging.

4 YOUR WHY AND YOUR MISSION

Know Your Why or Lose Your Way

"He who has a why to live for can bear almost any how."
- Nietzche

It has been said when you lose your Why, you lose your Way. Even in the old testament's book of Proverbs it states: "Where there is no vision, the people perish." So it is time to create your personal mission statement so you understand and reinforce your Why.

To recap where you should be in this journey, you should know:

☑ Your 5 natural strengths.
☑ Your primary and secondary advantages.
☑ Understand your Emotional Intelligence Quotient.
☑ Know your primary love language.
☑ Your life domains score and how healthy your life wheel is.
☑ Understand your roles in life and understand why they are important to you.
☑ Defined your Core Values.

A personal mission statement is a brief description what you want to focus on, what you want to accomplish, and what you want to become. It allows you to focus your energy, actions, behaviors, and decisions towards the things that are most important to you.

Writing a personal mission statement will create a vision for your life, for your career, for your family, for you personally, for what you want to accomplish. Your mission statement can be a two or three-word statement; it can be a full page as long as it defines what your mission is.

A personal mission statement:

• Characterizes the deepest and best within you.
• Utilizes your unique strengths and gifts.
• Is a mission bigger than yourself with a purpose of contribution.
• Is based on the principles to produce quality-of-life results (not standards of life).
• Provides value to others.
• Represents your significant roles in your life (your life wheel).
• It is written to inspire YOU!

Stephen Covey said – *"We don't invent our missions, we detect them."*

Your Mission Statement can make a major difference in your life. We all have a vision of where we are going but when you put a mission statement with a vision statement it clearly articulates where you are going and why. It brings focus and purpose to your life.

Your personal mission statement is a powerful tool because it provides you with a path for success, and it gives you permission to say no to the things that are distractions. It will change over time as we get older, we have more life experiences and acquire new skills. If your mission statement doesn't change, you can run the risk of it not being relevant to you.

To help you get started, below are some sample statements; my mission statement, and 5 others from people you may know. Some Examples of what has been included in other mission statements are:

• To bring beauty into people's lives.
• To contribute to society.
• To raise a great family that understands giving.
• To make a difference.
• To have peace.
• To create joy.
• To excel in my field.
• To help others move from success to significance.

MY MISSION STATEMENT

"To inspire others to move from success to significance by knowing their strengths, understanding their why and living on purpose to be better than they thought they could be."

5 SAMPLE MISSION STATEMENTS

DENISE MORRISON, CEO OF CAMPBELL SOUP COMPANY
 "To serve as a leader, live a balanced life, and apply ethical principles to make a significant difference."

In an interview Morrison said, "The personal mission statement was important for me because I believe that you can't lead others unless you have a strong sense of who you are and what you stand for. For me, living a balanced life means nurturing the academic, physical, and spiritual aspects of my life so I can maintain a sense of well-being and self-esteem."

JOEL MANBY, CEO OF HERSCHEND FAMILY ENTERTAINMENT

"I define personal success as being consistent to my own personal mission statement: to love God and love others."

Manby's company, Herschend Family Entertainment, owns and operates 26 family-oriented theme parks and attractions across the United States, including Dollywood and the Harlem Globetrotters. He told Skip Prichard that he achieves his personal mission statement in his own endeavors, but feels blessed to be able to achieve it in a growing, profitable business.

OPRAH WINFREY, FOUNDER OF OWN, THE OPRAH WINFREY NETWORK

"To be a teacher. And to be known for inspiring my students to be more than they thought they could be."

In an issue of O magazine, Winfrey recalls watching her grandmother churn butter and wash clothes in a cast-iron pot in the yard. A small voice inside of her told her that her life would be more than hanging clothes on a line. She eventually realized she wanted to be a teacher, but "I never imagined it would be on TV," she writes.

SIR RICHARD BRANSON, FOUNDER OF THE VIRGIN GROUP

"To have fun in [my] journey through life and learn from [my] mistakes."

Branson shared his personal mission statement in an interview with Motivated magazine. He added that "In business, know how to be a good leader and always try to bring out the best in people. It's very simple: listen to them, trust in them, believe in them, respect them, and let them have a go!"

AMANDA STEINBERG, FOUNDER OF DAILYWORTH.COM

"To use my gifts of intelligence, charisma, and serial optimism to cultivate the self-worth and net-worth of women around the world."

Steinberg launched DailyWorth in 2009 to help women build wealth. Since then, she's grown her site to more than 1 million subscribers. "I believe financially empowered women are the key to world peace," she says.

YOUR MISSION STATEMENT

You will need to write down multiple version until you feel comfortable owning it. It needs so support who you are, who you want to be, and what you want to accomplish. Make sure you allocate enough time to get this right.

PERSONAL MISSION STATEMENT INSTRUCTIONS
1. Follow the Steps 1 – 5 on the Mission Statement Worksheet.
2. Reflect on the 2 questions in Step 6.
3. Start working on your personal mission statement.
4. Create 3 – 10 personal mission statements
5. Select the 1 that fits you.

Mission Statement Worksheet

Step 1 - List your 5 Strengths (from Strengths Finders Assessment)

Step 2 - List your Advantages (from Fascination Assessment)

Step 3 – List your skills and your abilities (music, teaching, planning, etc.)

Step 4 – List your Core Values (from previous chapter)

Step 5 – List your Dreams and Passions (if money was not an object)

Step 6 – Write your Mission Statement
- What is the single thing you want to be remember for?
- What is the most important legacy I can leave to my family, friends, and colleagues?

My Mission Statement

A personal mission statement is a brief description of what you want to focus on, what you want to accomplish, and what you want to become. It will create a vision for your life, career, family and you personally.

5 YOUR PRIORITIES

What Really Matters to You?

"One day you will wake up and there won't be any more time to do the things you've always wanted. Do it now."
– Paulo Coelho

Now it's time to set some priorities for each of your life accounts. Life Accounts are unique to you and they depend on where you are in life. For instance, if you aren't married yet, you won't have a wife or husband account. Your life accounts will definitely change over time so don't try to think about the future right now, just define your current life accounts today.

Your accounts are interconnected because YOU are at the center of all of them. You can have a major life accounts like family, but it is better to break them down further like specific family members. This will help you when you are creating your life plan in the next chapter.

We can start by reviewing your life wheel and your roles you defined when you were defining your core values.

As a reminder, our Life Wheel had the following domains:

- Career
- Finances
- Health
- Family
- Romance
- Growth
- Fun
- Faith

Use these along with your roles you defined to list your priorities. As an example, my priorities are below.

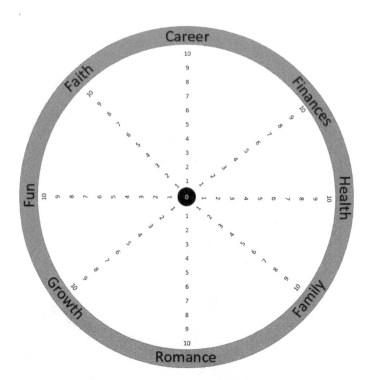

1. God
2. Me – Health, Growth, Rest
3. My Wife – Tanna
4. My Daughters – Abby, Allison, Emily
5. Extended Family
6. Friends
7. Career
8. Finances
9. Helping Others

I really struggled with me being second and above my wife and daughters. I read a lot on this and had to come to grips that if I wasn't taking care of myself, I could not take care of anyone else. The best example of this is when the flight attendant on an airplane states at the beginning of the flight that in the case of an emergency put your oxygen mask on first, then help others around you. It is the same thing when you are thinking about your priorities. If you aren't prioritizing you, you will have minimal effect on others.

"I can't help anyone unless I am taking care of myself"

PRIORITIES WORKSHEET INSTRUCTIONS
1. Review your Life Wheel Assessment.
2. Review your roles on your core values worksheet.
3. Create your priority list for each life account using the form below.
   Note, you may have to break out certain priorities like Me-Health, Me-Growth, and Me-Rest
4. Rate the current state of each priority

Priority of Life Accounts Worksheet

Priorities	Current State		
	Bad	OK	Great

So now that you have established your priorities and rated the, it's time to establish some rough goals and what you would like to see change for each priority. We will get specific and detailed when you create your life plan in the next chapter.

PRIORITIES IMPROVEMENT WORKSHEET INSTRUCTIONS

1. List your priority on the worksheet
2. Think about something you would like to change, improve, add to make that priority better
3. List that in the Improvements section
4. Repeat for each priority

Note – we will get specific about each priority in the next chapter

Priority Improvements Worksheets	
Priority	**Improvements (Quick Thoughts)**

Now that you have your priorities defined, we need explore if you have identified or can express your ONE BIG THING. Jim Collins calls this a BHAG – Big Hairy Audacious Goal — in his book Built to Last. Some may call them long-term goals, while others call it a moonshot (shot at the moon, not the other one).

BHAG's are bigger, bolder and more powerful than regular long-term goals. They are typically a 10 -30 year commitment, but they are exciting and tangible that just makes sense without a lot of details. Whatever you refer to it as, do you know what your BHAG is? If not, take a long term view and think about what you would like to accomplish. Something that you will be remembered for in a good way. Write yours below in the box.

BHAG – Big Hairy Audacious Goal

Take a breather before you start the next step. You are actually going to create your life plan. This is a big step toward living your life on purpose and intentionally. Living on purpose within your strengths and natural self with your core values defined, your personal mission statement defined, and your priorities defined, it's time to define your roadmap so you can be the best you that you can be.

Chapter Notes and Key Learning Points

If you are not prioritizing you, you will have minimal effect on others.

6 YOUR LIFE PLAN

Life on Purpose, with Purpose and a Plan

"You don't plan to fail
– you fail to plan"
– Craig Sroda

Creating your life plan is an important step. Use this template as a guide to help you document your life plan. Connecting your head and your heart through this process is an important realization, so stretch yourself in ways you never imagined.

Remember - "Your mind is like a parachute; it only works when it is open."

The sections of this template are:

• **Outcomes** - determining how you want to be remembered.
• **Priorities** - defining your priorities in life.
• **Action Plans** - putting together plans for your priorities and desired outcomes.

As Stephen Covey outlined in his book Seven Habits of Highly Effective People - "Begin with the End in Mind." The first step to defining your outcomes is by looking ahead to your envisioned future or future state. Some outcomes will require you to think about what people will say about you when you are dead and gone. Not that anybody wants you dead, but a lot of people have regrets when they are on their death bed. The whole point of doing this exercise is to minimize your regrets.

Please allocate intentional time to this. This means dedicate quiet time, think time, and process time. Try not to rush this and allow enough time to finish this version. Treat it as if it is your life - BECAUSE IT IS!!! Just one more reminder ... this should be reviewed and updated as needed because life is a journey and things change. Use your judgment as to creating the next version of this, but be intentional when your life does change.

Good Luck and Let's Get Started!!!

LIFE PLAN INSTRUCTIONS

1. List your priorities from the previous chapter with a summary of how you want to be remembered for each priority.
2. For each of your priorities complete one life plan worksheet with the following sections:
    - Your Why Statement – why is your role and responsibility for this priority.
    - Your Desired Future –what this priority looks like in a future state, in 5, 10, or 30 years.
    - Supporting Verse or Inspirational Quote –a bible verse or a quote that keeps you engaged with this priority. It can be a reminder of why this priority is important to you.
    - Where You Are Today – this is where you look in the mirror and bullet point out where you are today for this priority. (be honest with yourself)
    - Commitments – this is where you put specific actions to move you from where you are today to your desired future. Use bullet points and be specific. Any commitments or goals need to be S.M.A.R.T. (Specific, Measurable, Actionable, Realistic, Time-Bound (due date)).
3. You can make copies of the life plan worksheet for each priority or download the template from www.yoursweetspotbook.com.
4. Repeat for each priority.
5. Review your life plan with a friend.
6. Download the templates or copy the life plan priority planning worksheets for each of your priorities and create a binder. This will help on monthly checkups.

"You Never Hit a Target You Don't Have"

My priorities and outcomes worksheet are below along with one priority sample of a completed Life Plan Priority Planning Worksheet.

Priorities & Outcome sample

Priority	How You Want to Be Remembered
God	Faith was my foundation and it showed.
Self – Health	He was fit and pushed himself to keep growing from a health perspective till his last day. He lived an intentional health life with the actions to support it so he could help others.
Self - Growth	He was a forever learner in all areas of his life and liked to share with others so they could continually be improving themselves.
Self – Rest	He knew what refueled him and verified consistently so he was ready to help others.
Wife - Tanna	We grew together in many ways. Our paths were not straight, but he was commitment to helping us grow on our journey. He loved me unconditionally and helped me be a better women in many ways.
Daughter – Abby	He was a great dad that help me understand my foundation, listened to me for what I wanted, understood my uniqueness in the world, supported me in my life journey, demonstrated love by loving my mom, and helped me be better than I thought I could be.

Priorities & Outcome sample (Cont.)

Priority	How You Want to Be Remembered
Daughter – Allison	He was a great dad that help me understand my foundation, listened to me for what I wanted, understood my uniqueness in the world, supported me in my life journey, demonstrated love by loving my mom, and helped me be better than I thought I could be.
Daughter – Emily	He was a great dad that help me understand my foundation, listened to me for what I wanted, understood my uniqueness in the world, supported me in my life journey, demonstrated love by loving my mom, and helped me be better than I thought I could be.
Extended Family	He was a good brother/uncle that kept stretching himself to grow and impact us and others through his experiences.
Friends	He had the unique ability to have fun, work hard, and enjoy life to leave a positive ripple effect to impact others.
Career	He was a continuous learner and wanted everyone to be in their "sweet spot" where our passion and strengths intersected. He wanted us to be happy at work so we have a positive impact in our family, the community and the people around us.
Finances	He grew up from nothing, worked hard and kept pushing because he knew God had a plan for him even through his many trials. (James 1:2)
Helping Others	His mission was to help others be better than they thought they could be by helping them understand their strengths, their why, and their mission and purpose.

Life Plan Priority Planning Worksheet Sample (Wife - Tanna)

Your Why Statement
My why and purpose for Tanna is to be the most loving and trusted partner I can be. To prioritize her in my life and to care for her, have fun with her, grow with her for the rest of my live. I will respect and cherish her feelings, be slow to speak on bad days, and encourage on great days realizing everyday will not be as I planned, but as God has planned for us. I will support her in whatever she wants to pursue, give advice as a friend, and connect friends in our life that our trusted advisors to help us maintain a relationship of integrity, trust, pure friendship and love.
Your Desired Future
I am engaged with Tanna from ALL aspects of our life. She is my sounding board, partner, friend, and lover to help me work through ALL things. I am there for Tanna with ALL my head and heart and she has a comfort and trust she has never felt in her life. Our life is something others will look at and see total love. I am always excited to be with Tanna and respect our differences as they are gifts from God to make us complete.
We experience life together; we explore local and distant places, adventures, and support the community and our family with God as our third strand to keep us on his plan. We are stretching ourselves to grow to help and we are totally there for each other to fill us when the earthly things tear us down. Our unconditional love makes us strong, secure, and able to continue through tough times, but we remember this is of this world and God has plans for us to execute on every day.
Supporting Verse or Inspirational Quote
James 1:19 - My dear brothers and sisters, take note of this: Everyone should be quick to listen, slow to speak and slow to become angry, because human anger does not produce the righteousness that God desires.

Life Plan Priority Planning Worksheet (Wife-Tanna Sample Cont.)

Where You Are Today
<ul><li>I am working a little too much.</li><li>I am working on quarterly vacations with Tanna, but haven't been consistent.</li><li>I am consistent with date nights weekly but need to be fully engaged during the dates, even some preplanning to make them special.</li><li>I am more aware of her feelings, but need to separate what she is saying from what she is feeling.</li></ul>

Commitments
<ul><li>Consistent Dinner / Family time 3 nights a week during work week</li><li>Weekly date nights with Tanna</li><li>Treat her as my Princess (*with respect always*)</li><li>Annual Anniversary vacations</li><li>Summer R&R Fridays</li><li>Always be transparent with my schedule/life/thoughts</li><li>Share my financial plans (career and our future) for us so she is always aware</li><li>Make sure I am responsible with our finances and always let her know what I am thinking</li><li>Support her as life changes and continually ask God to protect our marriage, our relationship, and her as an individual.</li></ul>

Now it's your turn. Fill out the following worksheets.

Priorities and Outcomes Summary Worksheet	
Priority	**How You Want to Be Remembered**

Life Plan Priority Planning Worksheet

Priority	<fill in priority here>

Your Why Statement

Your Desired Future

Supporting Verse or Inspirational Quote

Where You Are Today

Commitments

At this point you should have identified your priorities, understand where you are now, and where you want to be in the future with each of them. It's time to put the commitments you made for each priority into action. As I stated before, "you don't plan to fail, you fail to plan". Take the time to create a binder of your life plan priority planning worksheets for each priority to keep close to you for quick reference. It is you're your life so treat it as gold or whatever you consider to be valuable or precious.

You don't plan to fail. You fail to plan. Make a plan for your life. Treat your life plan as gold or whatever you consider to be valuable or precious.

7 THE PLAYBOOK

Execution Plan for Your Life Journey

> "One can choose to go back toward safety or forward toward growth. Growth must be chosen again and again; fear must be overcome again and again"
> – Abraham Maslow

Now it is time to choose and execute. Before we dig in, it is important to realize your playbook will be a journey and not a destination. I used to think about goals and destinations which meant there was an end. Besides your death, there is another end to life that can start right now by putting together the plan for your life's journey from here forward.

I figured this out in my early 30's on a trip to see my brother in Green Bay Wisconsin. We had a Ford Expedition and I decided rather than stop at every gas station along the way for our three daughters to go to the bathroom, I would put a training "potty" in the back seat. This way when one of our daughters had to go to the bathroom, I would slow down, have my wife help them, and we would dump it out the window. Sounded like a great plan to me. We started on our journey from South Bend, Indiana and sure enough, when we hit Chicago it was time to try out my idea. Inside my head I was excited because this would allow us to get to Green Bay in record time. So all went well until I slowed down and my wife threw it out the window and it flew back in her face. Let's just say it was a quiet for the next four-hour ride. That is when I realized I need to enjoy the journey as much as the destination. Now when we go on vacation, we say a quick prayer in the garage and state out loud that the vacation begins now and the journey is part of the vacation—so let's go have fun.

Now it's time to act and execute your plan and live the priorities that are truly important to you. You will have to be watchful of the urgent things that come up in life as they can distract you from your true priorities. This will be your life journey as it is intended to be. There will be many milestones along the way, so the sooner you get to a mind-set that you are on journey and not seeking a destination, the more you will accomplish and enjoy your days and your life.

The commitments you made for each of your life plan priorities can be considered goals, targets, or milestones for your life. You have established commitments for each priority which is why they need deadlines and a roadmap. You never hit a target you don't have so let's get started.

EXECUTION PLAYBOOK

EXECUTION PLAYBOOK INSTRUCTIONS
1. Complete the One Page - Life Plan Playbook
2. Complete the Annual Goals Timeline
3. Complete a Weekly Plan for next week by life domain
4. Complete Weekly Reviews
5. Complete Quarterly Reviews (and adjust accordingly)

Templates are at the end of this chapter and downloadable Templates of these documents can be found at www.yoursweetspotbook.com.

Focus is a key to success as you define what success means for you. Just like the sun can start a fire when focusing its energy with a magnifying glass, you can make a difference with focus and discipline. Ensuring you are focusing on the important activities in your life, you need to start running your decisions through the decision matrix. This will help you accomplish the very things you put in your playbook and prioritize the right activities.

The following decision matrix will help you identify tasks that are time wasters and interruptions. We live in a world now of everything having the option of instant response which can cause you not to accomplish the important things in your life. I know some days will feel like you are just managing crises and putting out fire after fire. But the days and the tasks you can control, you should. Most of the time you are probably confusing the urgent with the important.

Quick Test – when your phone beeps, do you immediately look at it? Do you feel you have to respond to email immediately when you hear that ding? If so, you are indeed confusing the urgent with the important.

	URGENT	NOT URGENT
IMPORTANT	**Quadrant 1** important and urgent *Crises, deadlines, problems*	**Quadrant 2** Important but not urgent *Relationships, planning, recreation*
NOT IMPORTANT	**Quadrant 4** not important but urgent *Interruptions, meetings, activities*	**Quadrant 3** not important, not urgent *Time wasters, pleas- ant activities, trivia*

"What is important is seldom urgent and what is urgent is seldom important"

The Difference Between Urgent and Important

Urgent means the task requires immediate attention. These are the to-do's that shout out – NOW! Urgent tasks put us in a reactive mode which usually is a defensive, hurried, negative and narrow-focused mindset. Important means tasks that contribute to our long-term mission, values, and goals. Sometimes important tasks are also urgent, but typically they are not. When we focus on important activities we operate in a responsive mode, which helps us stay rational, calm, and open to new opportunities.

It's pretty intuitive distinction, yet most of us frequently fall into the trap of believing that all urgent activities are important. This mind-set originates from our ancestors where the urgent was important—like being chased by a saber-tooth cat because it could be the difference between life and death.

Like I mentioned earlier, the new technologies are constantly bombarding us like the dings of email, twitter, and texts. We are being conditioned to be in an "always-on" state and we have the high potential to lose sight of the truly important and our long term direction. Working with the decision tree and reviewing your playbook can help you avoid burnout and stagnation because you keep your long term objectives at the top of your mind.

Choose to RESPOND vs. REACT by understanding each quadrant outlined below.

QUADRANT 1: URGENT AND IMPORTANT TASKS

Quadrant 1 tasks are both urgent and important. These are the tasks that require our immediate attention and also work towards fulfilling our long-term goals and missions in life.

Quadrant 1 tasks typically consist of crises, problems, or deadlines. Here are a few specific examples of Urgent and Important tasks:
- Certain emails (new business opportunity that requires immediate action, critical decisions, etc.)
- Tax deadline
- You have a heart attack and end up in the hospital
- Spouse in emergency room
- Car doesn't start
- Household chores
- Child is in the principal's office

With a bit of planning and organization, many Q1 tasks can be made more efficient or even eliminated. For example, instead of waiting until your check engine light goes on, you take it in for routine maintenance. You can do this with projects at home and at work. This will allow you to an urgent and important task into just an urgent (Quadrant 2) tasks so you can plan accordingly. You won't be able to remove all urgent and important tasks but reducing them allows you to have more breathing room to be intentional about your time.

QUADRANT 2: NOT URGENT BUT IMPORTANT TASKS

Quadrant 2 tasks are the activities that don't have a pressing deadline, but help you achieve your important personal, and work goals as well as help you fulfill your overall mission.

Q2 tasks are typically centered around strengthening relationships, planning for the future, and improving yourself.

Here are some specific examples of Not Urgent but Important Tasks:
- Meditating
- Journaling
- Exercising
- Weekly planning
- Long-term planning
- Family time

- Reading for Growth in all your life domains
- Taking a class to improve a skill
- Spending time with a rewarding hobby
- Studying
- Date night with wife
- Creating a budget and savings plan

Stephen Covey stated we should seek to spend most of our time on Q2 activities, as they're the ones that provide us lasting happiness, fulfillment, and success. Unfortunately, there are a couple key challenges that keep us from investing enough time and energy into Q2 tasks:

- Fortunately, you completed your life plan and priorities in the previous chapter. Q2 is where your time should be spent to achieve what truly is important to you. This is the intentional and productive quadrant to live an intentional life.

- Our default mode is to focus on what is pressing most. Without deadlines it can be hard to get energized to spend time here, but with your quarterly goals and weekly planning sheets it will be in your current state of mind. Make sure you practice the SMART discipline when setting goals (Specific, Measurable, Actionable, Realistic, Time-Bound)

Q2 activities can be kept on "the list" forever without deadlines and actions to back them up. They can sometimes be on the someday list especially with the urgent things that keep popping up. Living intentionally and proactively will allow you to attack this list and accomplish what you set out to do. You have to have to shift your mindset to I am going to this done by X vs. I hope to get this done by Y. You need to commit, then execute.

QUADRANT 3: URGENT AND NOT IMPORTANT TASKS
Quadrant 3 tasks are activities that require our attention now but don't help us achieve our goals or mission. Most of these activities are helping others achieve their goals and priorities. Examples of these are:
- Text messages
- Phone calls
- Most emails (some emails could be urgent and important)
- Unplanned guests or family that wants your help with a project or chore
- Favors from a co-worker who just stop by during high productivity time
- Request from friends to help them with a project, advice, or just meetings about minor things

Stephen Covey stated many people spend most of their time on Q3 tasks and think they are working in Q1. The deceiving part of Q3 activities are they feel important because you are helping others out. That is not a bad thing but need to be balanced with Q2 activities.
Spending too much time in Q3 will give you the allusion you are getting a lot done but the fact will be shown you are not accomplishing any of your long-term goals. This will leave you very frustrated and help others at the expense of your own.
Learn to say No and use your priority list that you now have to help you. When a request comes in, run it through your priority list to see which activity will take priority – this will be the YES to my priorities and NO to theirs.

QUADRANT 4: NOT URGENT AND NOT IMPORTANT TASKS
Quadrant 4 activities aren't urgent and aren't important. They don't help you achieve your long-term goals or mission. Examples can be:
- Surfing the web for nothing
- Social Media browsing - Facebook, Twitter, Instagram
- Watching TV
- Playing video games
- Shopping to kill time
- Gambling

If we are honest with ourselves, we spend too much time in Q4 activities. We all have those moments when we get sucked into TV for news or a show, or surfing the internet and find out we just blew two hours or a whole morning. We can't eliminate these activities totally because sometimes these activities allow us to rest and regroup. The goal is to spend less than 5% of your waking hours in this Q4.

Filtering out everything coming our way is a new talent or skill that we have to develop further. We historically didn't have to do this or just didn't do it. So we must actively work on intentional filtering of all the noise.

Spending most of your time in Q2 (Not Urgent but Important) activities will energize you give you a sense of peace, control, and feeling of achievement. This will allow you to own your life and make real progress with the things you identified as important and a priority to you. Always be careful that other people's priorities don't become yours.

URGENT   NOT URGENT

IMPORTANT

QUADRANT 1:
important and urgent

1

QUADRANT 2:
important but not urgent

2

NOT IMPORTANT

QUADRANT 4:
not important but urgent

4

QUADRANT 4:
not important not urgent

3

THE WEEKLY EXECUTION RHYTHM AND REVIEW PROCESS

It is important to review your life plan weekly before you create your weekly plan using the weekly planning sheet. Reviewing your life plan playbook weekly will ensure your actions for the week are supporting and aligning with your quarterly, annual and even your BHAG goals. Getting into a weekly rhythm and making it a habit will be the difference from idea to achievement. The weekly execution rhythm steps are below.

WEEKLY EXECUTION RHYTHM CHECKLIST
1. Weekly Reviews and Planning for the Week (Sunday night)
a. Complete the Weekly Score Sheet
b. Complete the Weekly Plan
2. Review your Core Values and Mission Statement
3. Review your Priorities
4. Review your 1 year goals
5. Review your quarterly goals (if quarterly goals need to be adjusted, adjust them)
6. Schedule events in your calendar beyond your control
7. Schedule events in your calendar in your control that work toward your quarterly goals
8. Schedule everything else

On the following page, you will find a weekly rhythm checklist that you can copy to help you create your habit. A downloadable version can be found at *www.yoursweetspotbook.com*.

Other tools that I use and can be very helpful are your ideal week worksheet and your annual calendar worksheet. Samples of these tools can be found in this chapter, and blank copies can be downloaded from *www.yoursweetspotbook.com*. The purpose of your ideal week is to visualize and plan your ideal week. We all know we don't always have an ideal week but if we shoot for it we will be more productive because this is a proactive and intentional step not be in a reactive state.

The block calendar plan allows you to see your years by quarter. The first time I did this I was amazed at how much was already planned for my year ahead. Between school events, work events and social events there was a lot of the days that were already taken. What I like most about this tool is you can see your whole year by quarters and print it out so you can always have it with you. Even Microsoft Outlook which I use heavily, cannot show me my year this way which is an important part of making sure you are scheduling that activities that align you with your affirmed priorities.

Week of _____

WEEKLY RHYTHM CHECKLIST	
COMPLETED	**WEEKLY ACTION**
☐	Weekly Reviews and Weekly Plan (Sunday night)
☐	Review your Core Values and Mission Statement
☐	Review your Priorities
☐	Review your 1 year goals
☐	Review your quarterly goals *(if quarterly goals need to be adjusted, adjust them)*
☐	Schedule events in your calendar beyond your control
☐	Schedule events in your calendar in your control that work toward your quarterly goals
☐	Schedule everything else
NOTES	**JOURNAL/THOUGHTS FOR THE WEEK**

Sample of My Ideal Week

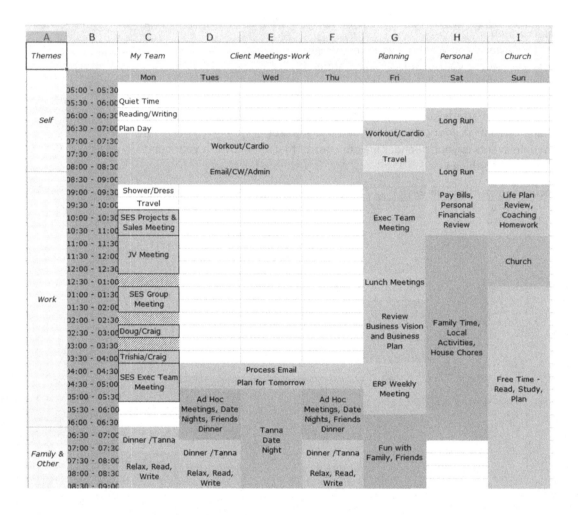

Sample of My Annual Calendar

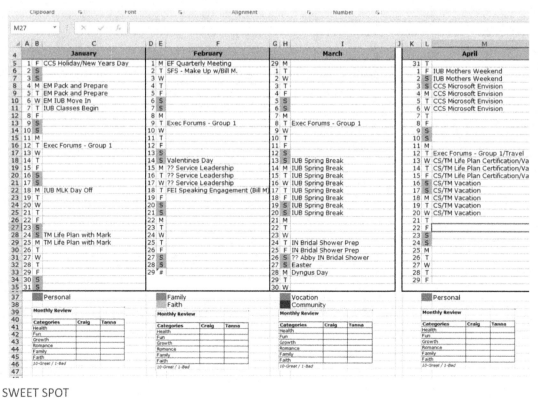

Congratulations!!!

You have just completed your life plan playbook so you can live on purpose, be intentional about your life, live with minimal regrets and live in your sweet spot. I highly suggest you get a 3 ring binder and keep all this information in one notebook for each year. Creating a new notebook per year will allow you to look back and see what progress you have made.

"Keep Separate Binders for Each Year"

Creating the life you want isn't a one-time thing, but a life long journey. Take joy in this process. When you are intentional about creating and living your life on purpose and in your sweet spot, your ripple effect can touch people you may never meet. You can create the positive energy in the world that helps others be better than they thought they could be.

That's enough talking. Now get to work and put your playbook into ACTION. And again, remember "We Don't Plan to Fail, We Fail to Plan."

Your playbook will be a journey and not a destination. Start your journey now by living with a plan and a purpose.

CRAIG SRODA lifeplan

MY LIFE JOURNEY PROFILE

Highs		Managed Hardware Store	Got Associates Degree	First Full-Time Job	Bought House	Graduated From Bethel	Started at Crowe	Bryan Aown Opened Bible	Married Tanna
Age		Teens				Twenties			
Lows	Mom Passed Away	Kicked Out of House							
Themes		Survive				Strive			

MY REPLENISHMENT CYCLE

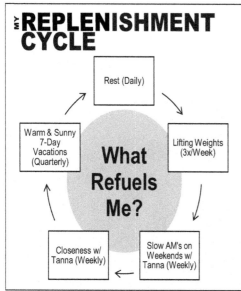

What Refuels Me?

- Rest (Daily)
- Lifting Weights (3x/Week)
- Slow AM's on Weekends w/ Tanna (Weekly)
- Closeness w/ Tanna (Weekly)
- Warm & Sunny 7-Day Vacations (Quarterly)

MY LIFE DASHBOARD

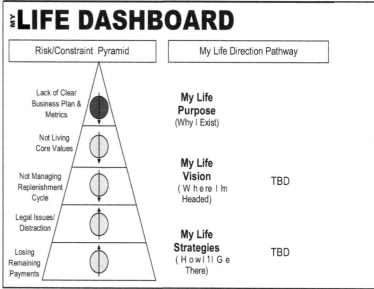

Risk/Constraint Pyramid

- Lack of Clear Business Plan & Metrics
- Not Living Core Values
- Not Managing Replenishment Cycle
- Legal Issues/ Distraction
- Losing Remaining Payments

My Life Direction Pathway

My Life Purpose (Why I Exist)

My Life Vision (Where I'm Headed) — TBD

My Life Strategies (How I'll Get There) — TBD

MY WIRING DASHBOARD

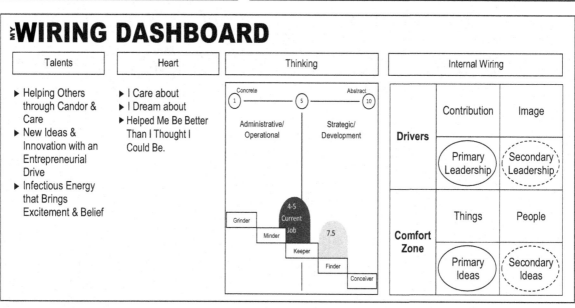

Talents
- Helping Others through Candor & Care
- New Ideas & Innovation with an Entrepreneurial Drive
- Infectious Energy that Brings Excitement & Belief

Heart
- I Care about
- I Dream about
- Helped Me Be Better Than I Thought I Could Be.

Thinking

Concrete 1 — 5 — Abstract 10

Administrative/ Operational — Strategic/ Development

Grinder, Minder, 4-5 Current Job, Keeper, 7.5, Finder, Conceiver

Internal Wiring

	Contribution	Image
Drivers	Primary Leadership	Secondary Leadership
	Things	People
Comfort Zone	Primary Ideas	Secondary Ideas

© Paterson Center, LLC.

Family Started	Baptized with Family	Business Start Up		New Leadership Awareness	Faith Re-Engaged	Hyatt Life Plan	Sold Business	Renewed Relationship w/ Tanna
				Thirties		Forties		
			Poor Life Decisions					
Grow				Blow Up		Rebuild		Relaunch

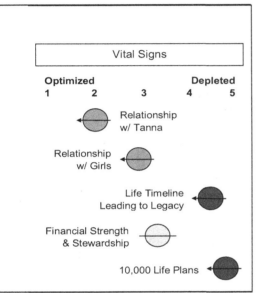

Vital Signs

Optimized				Depleted
1	2	3	4	5

Relationship w/ Tanna

Relationship w/ Girls

Life Timeline Leading to Legacy

Financial Strength & Stewardship

10,000 Life Plans

ᴹʸ ACCOUNTABILITY

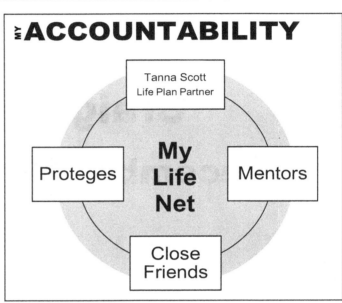

Tanna Scott
Life Plan Partner

Proteges

My Life Net

Mentors

Close Friends

ᴹʸ LIFE INITIATIVES PROFILE

Key	Objectives	Next Steps	Status	Start/ Completed Date(s)
1	Strategic Timeline for Key Steps in My Vocational Map	Create Excel Doc, Map in Target Dates, Discuss with Tanna & Team(s), Review Against Financial Model, Determine Date to Launch New Season	●	4/30/16 (Completed)
2	Develop Financial Model to Launch My Legacy/Vision	Living Budget, Future Expenses (Girls, Other), Retirement Projection, Financial Forecast for New Vocation, House Sold/ Estimate Price	●	1/15/16 (Completed)
3	Develop a Model to Complete 10,000 Life Plans by 2025	Mark/Craig/Josh Mtg., Potential Training in Indiana (Paterson Center), Business Plan Draft 1, Determine if GCC is Going to Move Forward	○	1/30/16 (Completed)
4	Build Business Plan to Integrate Legacy, Vocation, and Financial Models into Plan	Create Legal Entity, Certifications Complete, Develop/Gather Contacts, Fully on Board Exec. Forums, Develop Opportunity, Filter What to Say Yes or No To, Financial Model	●	4/30/16

© Paterson Center, LLC.

LIFEPLAN

Craig Sroda
December 15-16, 2015

By:
Mark Meyer

© Paterson Center, LLC.

BENEFITS OF LIFE PLANNING

- Comprehensive Perspective
  - Seeing My Life through the Lens of 5 Domains
  - My Story: Where Am I Now – Where Am I Headed
  - Full Picture, You are Content, Facilitated vs. Counseling

- Clarity/Focus
  - What are my True Values
  - Core Talents (Eph. 2:10)
  - What are My Next Steps? (W.I.N.S.)

- Integrity Inside & Out
  - Embrace the Truth about Myself
  - Taking Ownership of My Life
  - You have to Stand in Your Truth

- Breakthrough
  - Defining Moment
  - Unlocking/Releasing Me to My Next Level

- Surrendered
  - What is Keeping Me from Doing What God Says?
  - What's Holding Me Back?

- Change/Action
  - Doing the Hard Work
  - Plan the Work, Work the Plan, The Plan will Work

- Holy Spirit Process
  - He is With Us!

© Paterson Center, LLC.

LIFEPLAN PRINCIPLES

- **Perspective Before Planning**
    - A to B, Summit Viewpoint

- **Managing the Whole**
    - 5 Domains: Personal, Family, Vocational, Faith, Community

- **Facilitated vs. Prescribed/Counseling**
    - You are Content. I am Process.

- **Seek Truth**
    - Current & Emerging

- **Confidentiality**

- **You are Unique!**
    - The Scope of Heart, Talent - Vision

- **New Discipline**
    - Perspective > Plan > Execute > Review

LIFEPLAN OBJECTIVES

Domains	Specifics		Accomplished
Primary Objective	Clarity on My Legacy: "When I Look Back 100 Years From Now, What Will Matter?"		
Secondary Objectives	Personal	Clarity on Legacy – "When I Look Back 100 Years from Now What Will Matter?" ▶ Plan to Grow & Apply/Intellect ▶ Health, Hobbies, and Financial Integrated into Plan	
	Family	▶ Plan to Strengthen Relationship w/ Tanna ▶ Help Daughters Navigate Life – Model w/ Tanna, Strong Foundation	
	Vocational	▶ Clarity on Timeline for Career Decisions ▶ Financial Aligned to Timeline, Mission, and Strengths	
	Church	▶ How Do I Be More Respectful at Work? ▶ Plan – How Do I Get Closer to God?	
	Community	▶ Plan for Intentionality w/ Extended Family and Close Friends	

TURNING POINTS

Age	Specifics	Life Domain(s)
15	Mom Passed Away	
18	Kicked Out of House Managed Hardware Store – James Solomon	
20	Got Associates Degree	
21	First Full-Time Job: Housing Allowance Bought House	
23	BS at Bethel – No One Showed	
24	Started at Crowe	
25	Bryan Aown Opened Bible to Me/ GCC Married to Tanna	
26	Abby Born/Family	
27	Baptized with Family	
28	Business Start- Up	
38	Poor Life Decisions	
39	Faith Re-Engaged (Mark)	
41	New Leadership Awareness (Kem CD)	
43	Hyatt Life Plan	
45	Sold Business	
47	Renewed Vision for Relationship w/ Tanna	

© Paterson Center, LLC.

Theme	Survive			Strive				
Turning Points	Mom Passed Away (1981, 15)	Kicked Out of House (1985, 18)	Managed Hardware Store (1985, 18)	Got Associates Degree (1987, 20)	First Full-Time Job (1988, 21)	Bought House (1988-89, 21)	Graduated from Bethel (1991, 23)	Started at Crowe (1991, 24)
Personal	Loss, Had to Work vs. Play, Independence Kicked Off	Motivated – "Had to Get After It"	Listened to Tony Robbins & Other CD's	Moved to Next Level – New Milestone	Financial Relief, "Moved Up a Wrung," Eye Opening to White Collar	Felt Success/ Independent	Huge Achievement	Financial Step: 23-24K, Bought 2nd House
Family	Foundation Broken	Lived with Grandma, Cause Divide in Family – Held Grudge w/ Dad & Stepmom						Met Tanna
Vocational	Had to Get a Job (Martin's)	Motivated, Had to Earn More	Huge Learning Curve – Learning a "Trade" – Mechanical, Taught Mechanical Lessons		1st Full Time Job: $16,000			Big Step – Learned Management, Teamwork, Computer Skills, Innovation, Dots Connecting
Church		Usher at Church w/ Grandma, Some Sunday Consistency	James Solomon Kept Faith Visible – Opened Bible				Got First Big Bible – Didn't Know What It Meant	Kem/Don GCC, Connections, Don Sharing Faith
Community								1st "Give-Back" Initiatives

© Paterson Center, LLC.

Theme	Grow				Blow Up		
Turning Points	Bryan Aown Opened Bible (1992, 25)	Married Tanna (1992, 25)	Family Started (1992-96, 26)	Baptized with Family (1995, 27)	Business Start-Up (1996, 28)	Poor Life Decisions (1998-07, 30-39)	New Leadership Awareness (2007, 39)
Personal		Learning How to Share Life	Responsibility Realization Kicked-In, Financial Pressure		Stress, Ego Kicked In, Money Focus, Independence, Out-of-Balance	Drinking/ Alcohol, Narcissism Diagnosis, Bad Decision	New "Ah-Ha"
Family		Life Partner!	Tanna at Home Decision, Built 1st House (3rd House)	Tanna & I Decided Faith Part of Family	Gone a Lot, MIA, Strain on Relationship	Relationship w/ Tanna Lowest Point, Swapped Money for Time	
Vocational			Became a Manager – Still on Radar to Grow/Step Every 3 Years, Learned GP		Learnings: Sales, Consulting, General Business, Accounting, Account Management	Driven to Hit Numbers	CD From Kem – Andy Stanley
Church	Started Reading Bible, Small Group w/ Don	GCC Steps Together, Volunteering		External Step	Went Down	Started Tithing	New Faith Awareness
Community							

© Paterson Center, LLC.

Theme	Survive			Strive				
Turning Points	Mom Passed Away (1981, 15)	Kicked Out of House (1985, 18)	Managed Hardware Store (1985, 18)	Got Associates Degree (1987, 20)	First Full-Time Job (1988, 21)	Bought House (1988-89, 21)	Graduated from Bethel (1991, 23)	Started at Crowe (1991, 24)
Personal	Loss, Had to Work vs. Play, Independence Kicked Off	Motivated – "Had to Get After It"	Listened to Tony Robbins & Other CD's	Moved to Next Level – New Milestone	Financial Relief, "Moved Up a Wrung," Eye Opening to White Collar	Felt Success/ Independent	Huge Achievement	Financial Step: 23-24K, Bought 2nd House
Family	Foundation Broken	Lived with Grandma, Cause Divide in Family – Held Grudge w/ Dad & Stepmom						Met Tanna
Vocational	Had to Get a Job (Martin's)	Motivated, Had to Earn More	Huge Learning Curve – Learning a "Trade" – Mechanical, Taught Mechanical Lessons		1st Full Time Job: $16,000			Big Step – Learned Management, Teamwork, Computer Skills, Innovation, Dots Connecting
Church		Usher at Church w/ Grandma, Some Sunday Consistency	James Solomon Kept Faith Visible – Opened Bible				Got First Big Bible – Didn't Know What It Meant	Kem/Don GCC, Connections, Don Sharing Faith
Community								1st "Give-Back" Initiatives

© Paterson Center, LLC.

TURNING POINT LEARNINGS

#	Specifics
1	Having a Clear "Why" Matters
2	Simple Influences have had a Big Impact on My Life
3	I Need Conscious Life Priorities
4	Make Sure Whatever I Do, that It's Not Only about Me
5	Keep God My #1 Priority
6	I Need to Own My Responsibility of being a Great Husband and a Great Dad (Two of My Unique Roles)
7	I Need to Own My Life Decisions Based on My Priorities
8	Tanna has My Blind Spots. My Life Decisions are Our Life Decisions. She is a Filer with Full Veto Power.
9	I Need to Value Time Over Money
10	When I'm Disrespectful, I Need Dive into "What" is the Cause and Impact in My Life

© Paterson Center, LLC.

FOUR HELPFUL LISTS

Where Am I Today?	Today's Status	Controllability		
What's Right? (Optimize)		Full	Partial	None
Tanna & I	◐		✓	
Health	◐	✓		
Relationship w/ Daughter	◐		✓	
Morning Devotions	○	✓		
Progress w/ Life Plan	○	✓		
Learning	○	✓		
What's Wrong? (Fix)				
Environment at Current Job	●		✓	
Too Many Ideas, Too Many Plates Spinning	○	✓		
"I Feel Like I'm Building Someone Else's Dream"	●	✓		
What's Confused? (Clarify)				
What's My Role at Work?	○		✓	
Life Timeline	○	✓		
Life Goals	○	✓		
What is My Why?	○	✓		
GCC Engagement	●	✓		
House Logistics & Where We'll Live	○		✓	
Personal Brand	○	✓		
Vacation Rhythm	○	✓		
What's Missing? (Add)				
What's My Future Career	○	✓		
Mission Statement	●	✓		
Clear Legacy	●	✓		
Friends/Accountability Group	○		✓	
Financial Plan for Next Season	○	✓		

© Paterson Center, LLC.

TALENT-HEART ASSESSMENT

Categories			Specifics	Learnings
Talents (What)			▶ Helping Others through Candor and Care ▶ New Ideas & Innovation with an Entrepreneurial Drive ▶ Infectious Energy that Brings Excitement & Belief	<u>Personal</u> Affirms I'm Training and What I'm Learning is so that I can Help More People.
Clues		**Passions** What Do I Love to Do?	Helping People be Better and Find Their Wiring, Teaching, White Board, Brainstorming, Working Out, Learning	
		Drives What Fuels What I Do?	Growth; Helping Others; Seeing Tanna Grow; Girls Navigating New Chapters; If I Believe in Something, I'm After It	<u>Family</u> Excited about Helping Tanna w/ Her Life Plan and Certification
		Obsessions What Do I Constantly Think About?	What Can I Do to be Helpful in My Writing, Speaking, and Other means to Help People? How to Stay Connected w/ Tanna & Girls, New Ideas	
		Qualities How Others Describe What I'm Good At?	Technology/Whiteboards, Facilitating/Teaching, Mentoring – Teach Around Strengths, Genuinely Caring, Willing to Drive into Tough Conversations, Candid, "Draw People"	<u>Vocational</u> Where I'm Applying My Heart & Talents is a Miss Right Now (Pinnacle), Executive Forums is a "Fit"
		Longings What Must I Do or Overcome in My Life?	Great Husband, Great Dad, Stay Healthy, Build Something Great that I'm Proud Of – Business w/ Legacy, Mentoring App?	
		Spiritual Gifts How has God Used Me?	Evangelism in a "Normal" Way, Leadership, "Helps"	<u>Faith</u> There's Room for Growth – Limited Intentionality Outside of Devotions
		Strengthfinders What are my Five Themes?	Futuristic, Strategic, Achiever, Focus, Responsibility	
		Achievements What are My Proud Accomplishments?	Maverick Leader, Pioneering, Entrepreneurial	<u>Community</u> Room for Growth

© Paterson Center, LLC.

MY HEART

What I Care About?	What I Dream About?	Opus Gloris (How I Hope Others Describe Me When I Die?)
Helping Ppl Navigate Life, Strengths, Passion, and Living on Purpose My Marriage/Tanna Daughters Friends Be a Positive Influence Financial Freedom Intentional with My Life Legacy without Ego	How Many LifePlans can Tann & I Do in My Lifetime? Seeing the Country w/ Tanna Being Engaged w/ Daughter's Families Positive Grandparent Continued Strengthening of Relationship w/ Tanna (and Influence Others)	"He Help Me Be Better Than I Thought I Could Be."

© Paterson Center, LLC.

THINKING WAVELENGTH

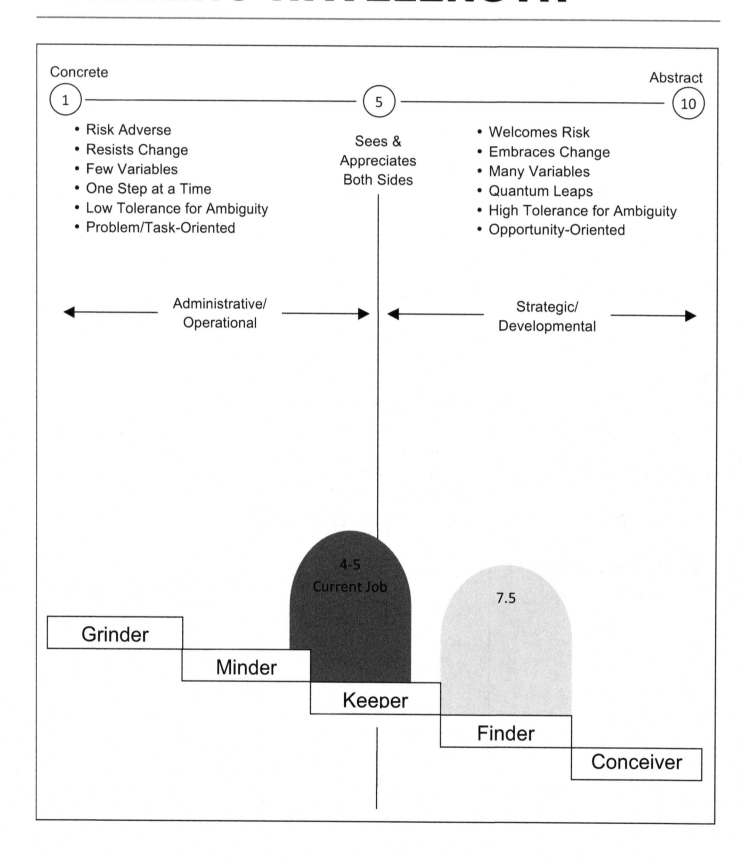

Concrete

Abstract

1 ——————————— 5 ——————————— 10

- Risk Adverse
- Resists Change
- Few Variables
- One Step at a Time
- Low Tolerance for Ambiguity
- Problem/Task-Oriented

Sees & Appreciates Both Sides

- Welcomes Risk
- Embraces Change
- Many Variables
- Quantum Leaps
- High Tolerance for Ambiguity
- Opportunity-Oriented

← Administrative/ Operational →

← Strategic/ Developmental →

4-5
Current Job

7.5

Grinder

Minder

Keeper

Finder

Conceiver

© Paterson Center, LLC.

INTERNAL WIRING

Drivers	Contribution	Image
	Primary Leadership	Secondary Leadership
Comfort Zone	Things	People
	Primary Ideas	Secondary Ideas

© Paterson Center, LLC.

TALENTS/THEMES

- Family Focus
- Value of Time
- Helping Others (and Career Component)

- Coaching/Facilitating
- Ideas/Innovation – "The Meaning of Me"
- Wanting Things to be Better
- Non-Offensive Candor
- Constructive Criticism
- Faith Included
- Infectious Energy – Get Excited, See Passion, Belief
- Not Afraid of Change/Risk
- Entrepreneurial

OPPORTUNITY MATRIX

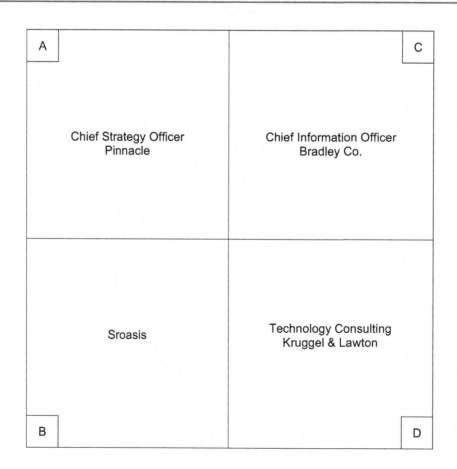

A	C
Chief Strategy Officer Pinnacle	Chief Information Officer Bradley Co.
Sroasis	Technology Consulting Kruggel & Lawton
B	D

© Paterson Center, LLC.

LIFE PERSPECTIVE FILTER

"One Red and It's Dead"	A	B	C	D
Experiences	⬤	⬤	⬤	⬤
Talent	◯	⬤	⬤	⬤
Heart	⬤	⬤	⬤	◯
Thinking	◯	⬤	◯	⬤
Wiring	◯	⬤	◯	◯
Values	⬤	⬤	⬤	⬤
Pathway	⬤	◯	⬤	◯
Results	X		X	

© Paterson Center, LLC.

VOCATIONAL GATING

Gates	A	B	C	D
Major Gates (Deal Breakers) ▶ Autonomy/Trust/ Work from Home ▶ No More than 5 Hours Away (Alone) a Month ▶ Positive, Leadership, Trusted Culture ▶ No Conflict w/ Note & Non-Compete ▶ Compensation 120K, 40-45 Hr. Work Week ▶ 6 Weeks PTO ▶ Non-Compete No Longer than 12 Mo.'s				
Major Gate Results	◯	◯	◯	◯
Minor Gates (Nice, But Not Critical…Tie-Breakers)				
Minor Gate Results	◯	◯	◯	◯

© Paterson Center, LLC.

WHAT BECAME CLEARER OVERNIGHT?

▶ My Legacy and Long Term Vision Matters – Time is Short.

▶ "If Money was No Object, What Would You Want to Do?"

▶ Affirmed the Lack of Passion <u>Where</u> I'm Working.

▶ Importance of Having a Financial Plan So I Know What Options I Have.

REPLENISHMENT CYCLE

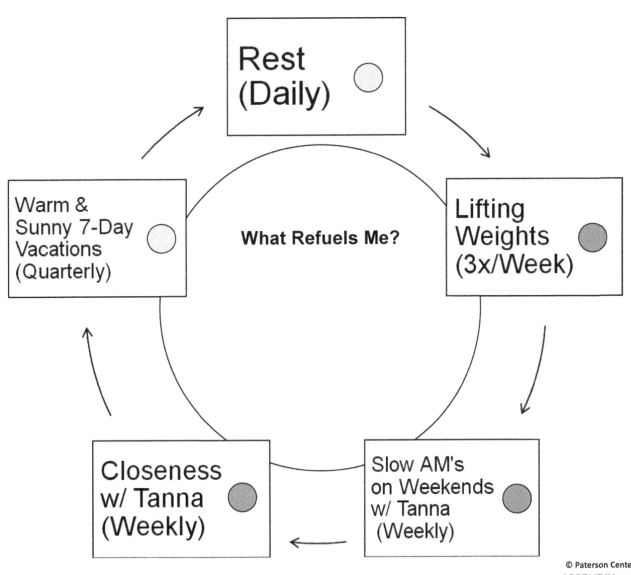

© Paterson Center, LLC.

REPLENISHMENT LONGLIST

▶ Open Weekends

▶ Slow Mornings on Weekends w/ Tanna

▶ Date Nights

▶ 7-Day Warm & Sunny Vacations

▶ Working Out/Exercise (Weights)

▶ Learning – (So That) Help Others

▶ Rest (Min. 7 Hrs Sleep)

▶ Fishing

▶ Camp Fires

▶ Hiking

▶ Mechanical/Working with Hands/Projects

▶ Devotions

▶ Closeness with Tanna

LIFE PURPOSE WORKSHEET

Verbs		Nouns
Touch	▶ "He Helped Me Be Better Than I Thought I Could Be"	Family
Help		Friends
Live		Community
Pioneer	▶ Help People Reach Their Potential with Inspiration, Ideas and Belief	Purpose
Improve		People
Drive		"The Why"
Inspire	▶ Energize Others to Live Out Their Unique Purpose	Ideas
Believe		"Sweet Spot"
Achieve		Energy
Innovate	▶ Inspire Others to Live on Purpose	Real
Teach		Fun
Infect		Others
Love	▶ Inspire Others to Live an Intentional Life	Relationship
Build		Growth
Grow		Foundation
Energize		Potential
Find		Intentional
Encourage		

I Exist to…

Inspire Others to Live an
Intentional Life

© Paterson Center, LLC.

VISION LONGLIST

Personal

- Still Working Out (16.5-17" Arms, Weights/Cardio 5-6x/Week
- Waist 32-33
- How Much Money is Enough?
- My Health Comes Before Vocation
- I Will Be Managing My Replenishment Cycle Well

Vocational

- Life Plan/Coaching Business and/or
- Business Consulting
- Technology
- StratOp
- How Many Life Plans
- Vocation is About Purpose Now
- Why I Work: Provide Financial Support, To Help Fuel My Other Domains, Stay in the Game, Build Relationships, To Ultimately Fulfill My Mission

Family

- Strong, Fun Relationship w/ Tanna
- Seeing Kids and Strong Relationship Wherever They Go/Live
- My Family "Rock" and Use of Time Comes Before The Vocational "Rock"
- Fund Established for Grandkids College Fund and Other Give-Back Initiatives

Faith

- 10,000 LifePlans Done by Me of Others in the Faith Community

Community

- Create Tools (Possibly App) to Help People Live Intentionally and Monitor Life Plan (w/ Mentoring)
- Paterson Center Partnership?

MY LIFE STRATEGIES

Personal

- Regularly Monitor My Replenishment Cycle
- Have a Functioning Financial Model
- Maintain Full Visibility to My Domains, Calendar, and Resources

Vocational

- Strategic Timeline in Place
- Business Plan with Budget
- Life Plan & StratOp Certified
- Engaged in Business Community to Build Relationships and Opportunities (Executive Forums, Other)
- Lifetime Learner to Continue to Add Values to Others

Family

- Maintain My Family as My #1 Filter in What I Do, How I Schedule, and Spend My Time

Faith

- Build and Execute Plan for 10,000 LifePlans

Community

- Develop Strategic Partnerships to Build Tools and Accomplish LifePlans Goal

© Paterson Center, LLC.

CORE VALUES

Values	Specifics
Prioritize Family	
Live Intentionally	
Have Fun	
Learn Forever	
Respect Others	

RISKS & VITAL SIGNS

Risks	Vital Signs
Losing Remaining Payments	Working Out
Legal Issues/Distraction	Financial Strength & Stewardship
Not Managing Replenishment Cycle	10,000 LifePlans
	Training/Learning/Certifications
Not Living Core Values	Relationship with Tanna
Lack of Clear Business Plan & Metrics	Relationship with Girls
	Life Timeline Leading to Legacy

© Paterson Center, LLC.

MY LIFE DASHBOARD

Risk Pyramid	Life Pathway		Vital Signs
Lack of Clear Business Plan & Metrics / Not Living Core Values / Not Managing Replenishment Cycle / Legal Issues/ Distraction / Losing Remaining Payments	**My Life Purpose** (Why I Exist)	"Inspire Others to Live an Intentional Life"	Optimized 1 2 3 / Depleted 4 5 — Relationship w/ Tanna — Relationship w/ Girls — Life Timeline Leading to Legacy — Financial Strength & Stewardship — 10,000 Life Plans
	My Life Vision (Where I'm Headed)	(See Long List)	
	My Life Strategies (How I'll Get There)	(See Long List)	

ACTION ITEMS LONGLIST

- ► Strategic Timeline for Vacation

- ► Timeline for Legacy

- ► Business Plan (Legal Entity)

- ► 10,000 LifePlan (Mark/Craig Mtg.)

- ► Financial Model Developed

- ► Schedule Vacations(s)

- ► Family Legacy Plan

- ► Schedule 2016 Visit(s) w/ Girls, Brad

- ► Create a List of Key Relationships

- ► Plan for Tools to Help LifePlan/Coaching (Tech & Others)

ACTION W.I.N. WHEEL

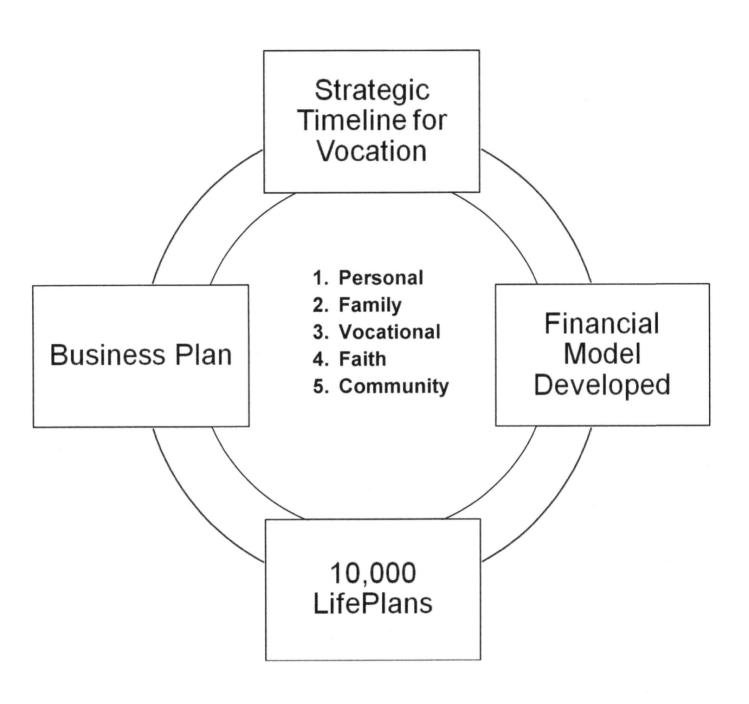

Strategic Timeline for Vocation

Business Plan

Financial Model Developed

10,000 LifePlans

1. Personal
2. Family
3. Vocational
4. Faith
5. Community

LIFE INITIATIVES PROFILE

Key	Objectives	Next Steps	Status	Start/ Completed Date(s)
1	Strategic Timeline for Key Steps in My Vocational Map	Create Excel Doc, Map in Target Dates, Discuss with Tanna & Team(s), Review Against Financial Model, Determine Date to Launch New Season	●	4/30/16 (Completed)
2	Develop Financial Model to Launch My Legacy/Vision	Living Budget, Future Expenses (Girls, Other), Retirement Projection, Financial Forecast for New Vocation, House Sold/ Estimate Price	●	1/15/16 (Completed)
3	Develop a Model to Complete 10,000 Life Plans by 2025	Mark/Craig/Josh Mtg., Potential Training in Indiana (Paterson Center), Business Plan Draft 1, Determine if GCC is Going to Move Forward	○	1/30/16 (Completed)
4	Build Business Plan to Integrate Legacy, Vocation, and Financial Models into Plan	Create Legal Entity, Certifications Complete, Develop/Gather Contacts, Fully on Board Exec. Forums, Develop Opportunity, Filter What to Say Yes or No To, Financial Model	●	4/30/16

LIFEPLAN TIME ASSESSMENT

Key Assumptions:

- ▶ 12 Hours/Day
- ▶ 7 Days/Week
- ▶ 4.33 Weeks/Month
- ▶ Total of 364 Hours Each Month

Life Domain	Hours/Month		% of Month		Notes
	Current	Proposed	Current	Proposed	
Personal	36	36	10%	10%	▶ Discounted LifePlans through Church in Faith Domain
Family	91	91	25%	25%	
Vocation	226	206	62%	57%	
Faith	7	27	2%	7%	
Community	4	4	1%	1%	
Totals	**364**	**364**	**100%**	**100%**	

WEEKLY LIFEPLAN

Date:		Family:	Hours:
Work:	**Hours:**		
		Faith:	**Hours:**
Personal:	**Hours:**		
		Community:	**Hours:**

© Paterson Center, LLC.

LIFENET

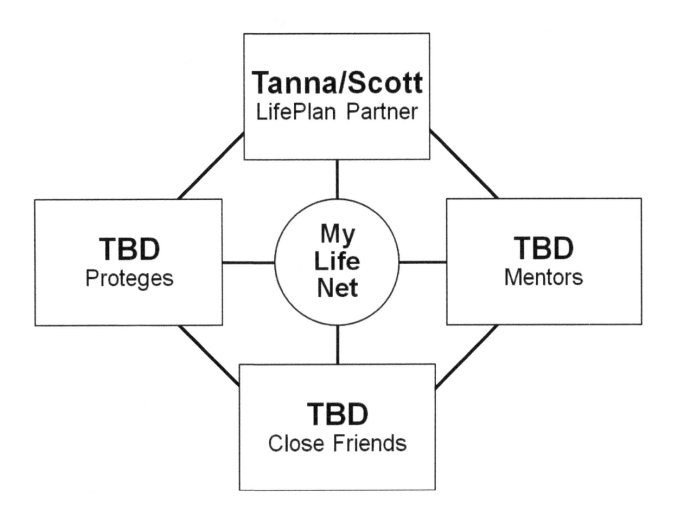

FAMILY ENGAGEMENT PLAN

	How We Will Live, Grow, Play Together	
Tanna		**Our Objectives:**
Abby		
Allison		**Our Values:**
Emily		
Together		

© Paterson Center, LLC.

LIFEPLAN LEARNINGS

- Legacy Clarity

- Vision Clarity

- Heat/Talent Dialed In – "What's Going to Make Me Happy?"

- Identifying What We Have Control Over

- Defining Core Values Identified

- Clarity of Mission

- Life Gates/Filters

- Replenish Reminder – What Refuels Me

- Importance of Having a Plan

- Merging Legacy/Values/Mission to Timeline

- Move from "Have To" To "Get To"

FINAL WORDS

- Congrats!

- It's a Journey, Not an Event

- Work the Plan

- Embrace Your Life Net

- I.D. Your LifePlan Partner

- Follow-Up Call

- God is With You!

© Paterson Center, LLC.

Printed in the United States
By Bookmasters